The
Four Seasons
Cookbook

BY NANCY ELMONT

Dorison House Publishers/Boston

The Author

A professional Home Economist, Nancy Elmont has a degree from Ohio State University. She has worked as a Test Kitchen Director at Kenyon & Eckhardt, the large advertising agency, as well as for hotel, hospital and university food services. She has acted as a consultant and food photography stylist, and has done exclusive home catering in the Boston area. To the delight of family and friends, she enjoys planning and serving wonderful meals all year 'round.

Copyright © 1981 by Dorison House Publishers, Inc.

Published by Dorison House Publishers, Inc.
824 Park Square Building
Boston, MA 02116

ISBN: 0-916752-47-X

Library of Congress Number: 80-70101

Manufactured in the United States of America

Contents

Foreword

In every country, seasons have influenced cuisine. The kind of food available at the marketplace determines what comes to the table. Even with today's rapid transportation and modern preserving methods making more foods year 'round possibilities, the flavor of fresh foods at their peak usually can't be surpassed, and discriminating cooks will choose them whenever possible. With that in mind, this cookbook is planned with menus and recipes that take advantage of foods when they are abundant and at their best at each season of the year in most parts of the United States.

There are forty menus with recipes divided among each of the four seasons. To welcome springtime there's a lamb dinner with melon and fresh asparagus. Fresh strawberries and pineapple are exciting spring fruits. Kabobs on the grill is a favorite summer treat with frosty cucumber soup, corn on the cob and watermelon guaranteed to relieve the heat. Autumn and winter appetites prefer heartier fare, so look for hot soups, cider, roasts, stews and pumpkin or apple desserts to bring warmth when the air is brisk.

Some of the menus are meant for everyday family meals, and others for entertaining small or large groups. They are intended to be used as guides to seasonal foods, and complementary combinations. I have prepared and tasted each of the dishes and selected the ones my family, friends and I enjoy most. I hope you, the reader, will try them or create variations of them for the sheer pleasure of cooking according to the four seasons.

Nancy Elmont

Spring

Melon Au Porto

Cut melon into bite-size chunks. For interest, select two or three kinds of melon.

6 cups cut up melon (cantaloupe, honeydew, watermelon)
½ cup port wine

Chill melon thoroughly. Spoon into individual serving dishes. Pour port over each serving.

Makes 6 servings.

Roast Rack of Lamb

The fragrance of the cooking roast will invite guests to the dinner table.

½ cup Dijon-type prepared mustard
¼ cup vegetable oil
1 garlic clove, minced
1 teaspoon dried rosemary leaves
½ teaspoon salt
1 (8-rib) rack of lamb

In a small bowl, stir together prepared mustard, vegetable oil, garlic, rosemary and salt; set aside.

Place lamb, fat side up, on rack in an open roasting pan. Coat meat with mustard mixture. Roast at 325° F. for 1½ hours or until meat is cooked to desired degree of doneness. (Internal temperature 165° F. for medium; 170 to 180° F. for well-done).

Makes 4 servings.

MENU

Melon Au Porto

Roast Rack of Lamb

New Potatoes With Sour Cream

Asparagus with Lemon Crumbs

Pineapple–Orange Chiffon Cake

New Potatoes with Sour Cream

Fresh little new potatoes are best when steamed in their skins just before eating and only until tender.

12 small new potatoes
1 cup sour cream
chopped chives

Remove a thin strip of peel around each potato. Steam in a saucepan until tender; drain. Serve potatoes topped with a dollop of sour cream and a sprinkling of chopped chives.

Makes 4 servings.

Asparagus with Lemon Crumbs

Lemon is the perfect complement for fresh asparagus.

2 lbs. fresh asparagus
3 tablespoons butter or margarine
¼ teaspoon grated lemon rind
2 teaspoons lemon juice
½ cup fine, dry bread crumbs
1½ teaspoons chopped parsley
¼ teaspoon salt

Trim and cook asparagus in rapidly boiling salted water until tender; drain. Meanwhile, melt butter in small saucepan. Remove from heat and stir in lemon rind, lemon juice, bread crumbs, parsley and salt. Serve seasoned crumbs over cooked asparagus.

Makes 4 servings.

Pineapple-Orange Chiffon Cake

Here's a light cake that is delicious as is or may be served with a crushed pineapple topping.

1 cup egg whites, at room temperature (8 egg whites)
½ teaspoon cream of tartar
1⅔ cups sugar, divided
2¼ cups cake flour
¾ cup unsweetened pineapple juice
½ cup vegetable oil
5 egg yolks
1 tablespoon baking powder
1½ teaspoons grated orange peel

In a large bowl, beat egg whites and cream of tartar with a mixer at high speed until soft peaks form. Gradually add ½ cup sugar, 1 tablespoon at a time, beating at high speed until sugar is completely dissolved and whites stand in stiff peaks. Set aside.

In another bowl, beat 1 cup sugar with flour, juice, oil, egg yolks, baking powder and orange peel at medium speed until well blended. Spoon whites over mixture and gently fold together, using rubber spatula.

Pour batter into ungreased 10-inch tube pan and bake for 1¼ hours at 325° F. or until top springs back when lightly touched. Invert cake pan; cool.

Makes 1 cake.

MENU

Melon Au Porto

Roast Rack of Lamb

New Potatoes With Sour Cream

Asparagus with Lemon Crumbs

Pineapple–Orange Chiffon Cake

Glazed Baked Ham

For an attractive garnish and extra flavor, dot ham with whole cloves.

3/4 cup honey
2 tablespoons prepared mustard
1 (12 to 14 lb.) smoked ham

In a small bowl, stir together honey and mustard; set glaze aside.

Place ham, fat side up, on a rack in an open roasting pan. Roast at 325° F., uncovered, for 3½ to 4½ hours or until meat thermometer reaches 160° F. About 20 to 30 minutes before ham is done, brush with the glaze and return to oven. Baste one more time before ham is finished cooking. Carve.

Makes 25 to 30 servings.

Scalloped Potatoes

For a special topping, stir together ½ cup fine, dry bread crumbs and 3 tablespoons melted butter; sprinkle over potatoes before baking.

8 tablespoons butter or margarine, divided
1 cup chopped onion
6 tablespoons flour
2 teaspoons salt
¼ teaspoon ground pepper
3 cups milk
8 medium potatoes, peeled and thinly sliced

In a saucepan over moderate heat, melt 6 tablespoons butter. Add onion and cook until onion is transparent. Add flour, salt and pepper and continue cooking for 4 minutes, stirring continuously. Gradually stir in milk and cook, stirring, until mixture thickens.

In a buttered 4-quart casserole, arrange half of the potatoes; pour half of the sauce over those potatoes. Repeat, making layers. Sprinkle the top with paprika and dot with remaining butter. Bake at 375° F., covered, for 45 minutes. Uncover and bake for an additional 15 minutes.

Makes 12 servings.

Sautéed Whole Green Beans

Simmer green beans only until they are just tender-crisp.

3 lbs. fresh whole green beans, ends trimmed
6 tablespoons butter or margarine
1½ cups sliced water chestnuts
6 teaspoons lemon juice
¾ teaspoon salt
¼ teaspoon ground pepper

Cook beans until tender in a saucepan in rapidly boiling salted water; drain. Melt butter in a fry pan. Add beans and water chestnuts; cook over moderate heat, stirring, for 3 minutes. Add lemon juice, salt and pepper and continue cooking for another minute.

Makes 12 servings.

Chiffonade Salad

Beet and egg give this salad both interesting flavor and color.

2 small or 1 large head Boston lettuce, washed and chilled
1 head romaine, washed and chilled
1 cup cooked beets, cut into strips
3 eggs, hard-cooked and sliced
12 tablespoons vegetable oil
¼ cup wine vinegar
¾ teaspoon salt
¼ teaspoon ground pepper
3 teaspoons chopped chives
3 teaspoons minced onion

In a large bowl, tear lettuces into bite-size pieces. Top with beets and egg slices. In a small bowl, stir together oil, vinegar, salt, pepper, chives and onion. Pour over salad mixture. Toss gently.

Makes 12 servings.

MENU

Glazed Baked Ham

Scalloped Potatoes

Sautéed Whole Green Beans

Chiffonade Salad

Meringue Shells with Marinated Strawberries

Meringue Shells with Marinated Strawberries

Meringue shells can be prepared a few days before serving, if stored in a dry place.

Meringue Shells:

6 egg whites, at room temperature
⅓ teaspoon cream of tartar
1½ cups sugar
⅓ teaspoon vanilla extract

Marinated Strawberries:

2 pints fresh strawberries, hulled and halved
6 tablespoons sugar
6 tablespoons Triple Sec or Cointreau or Grand Marnier
1 pint heavy cream
1 teaspoon vanilla extract
4 tablespoons powdered sugar

In a large bowl, beat egg whites with cream of tartar at high speed of mixer until soft peaks form. Gradually add sugar, 1 tablespoon at a time, beating after each addition until sugar is dissolved. It will take 10 to 15 minutes to incorporate all the sugar. Finally, beat in vanilla. Egg whites should form stiff peaks.

Spoon meringue into 12 mounds on greased baking sheet. Shape each mound into a 4-inch circle, making a nest in the center. Bake at 200° F. for 3½ hours. Do not allow shells to brown.

In a bowl, stir strawberries with sugar and Triple Sec. Allow to steep refrigerated, for 1 to 2 hours before serving.

Whip heavy cream in a bowl with vanilla extract and powdered sugar.

To serve, spoon strawberries into meringue shells. Top with a spoonful of whipped cream.

Makes 12 servings.

Stuffed Veal Breast

This cut of meat is not frequently served, but it is moist, tender and delicious when properly prepared.

4 tablespoons butter or margarine
½ cup chopped onion
⅓ cup chopped carrot
⅓ cup chopped celery
¼ lb. fresh mushrooms, washed and sliced
1½ cups fresh bread crumbs
1 teaspoon salt
¼ teaspoon ground pepper
1 (4 to 5 lb.) veal breast with pocket
1 cup dry white wine or dry vermouth
2 teaspoons cornstarch
1 teaspoon cold water

Melt butter in saucepan over moderate heat. Add onion, carrot and celery, cooking until tender. Stir in mushrooms and continue cooking for 3 to 5 minutes. Remove from heat. Stir in bread crumbs, salt and pepper.

Into the pocket of veal breast, lightly stuff crumb mixture. Secure the opening with food picks. Place veal in a large open roasting pan. Pour in wine. Cover pan and bake at 325° F. for about 3 hours or until meat is tender.

In a small bowl, stir together cornstarch and water; set aside. Remove veal from the roasting pan and strain cooking liquid into a saucepan. Place over moderate heat and add cornstarch mixture. Cook until the liquid comes to a boil and thickens. Carve veal breast and serve with sauce.

Makes 8 servings.

MENU

Stuffed Veal Breast

Maple Glazed Carrots

Broccoli Polonaise

Caesar Salad

Cognac Broiled Grapefruit

Maple Glazed Carrots

A very simple and interesting glaze for carrots.

1 lb. fresh carrots, cleaned and cut into coins
1 tablespoon butter or margarine
2 tablespoons maple syrup

In a saucepan, cook carrots in rapidly boiling salted water until tender; drain. Add butter and maple syrup to carrots in saucepan. Cook over moderate heat until syrup is reduced by half; serve.

Makes 4 servings.

Broccoli Polonaise

An elegant topping on the broccoli can turn this into a company side dish.

**1 bunch fresh broccoli (about 1½ lbs.), cleaned and
    trimmed into spears**
5 tablespoons butter or margarine
½ cup fine, dry bread crumbs
1 tablespoon lemon juice
1 egg, hard-cooked and finely chopped
1 tablespoon minced parsley
¼ teaspoon paprika

Cook broccoli in rapidly boiling salted water until tender; drain. Meanwhile, melt butter in a small saucepan; remove from heat and stir in bread crumbs, lemon juice, egg, parsley, and paprika. Sprinkle bread crumb mixture over cooked broccoli.

Makes 4 servings.

Caesar Salad

Save some fuss of making Caesar salad by preparing the dressing in the blender or food processor.

3 anchovy fillets
2 garlic cloves, peeled
3 tablespoons lemon juice
4 tablespoons oil
1 egg, coddled for 30 seconds
¼ teaspoon salt
dash ground pepper
1 medium head romaine, cleaned and chilled
1 cup croutons
¼ cup grated Parmesan cheese

In the cup of a blender or food processor, puree anchovies, garlic, lemon juice, oil, egg, salt and pepper; set aside. Tear romaine into bite-size pieces and place in bowl, layered with croutons and cheese. Pour dressing over romaine; toss and serve.

Makes 6 servings.

Cognac Broiled Grapefruit

This light dessert suits both family and company.

2 large grapefruits, halved, seeded, and sectioned
3 tablespoons honey
1½ tablespoons cognac

Place grapefruit halves on baking sheet. Drizzle with honey and sprinkle with cognac. Cook in preheated broiler for 10 minutes or until golden and heated through.

Makes 4 servings.

Hot and Sour Soup

This soup is very popular at Chinese restaurants.

¼ cup ground pork
1 teaspoon dry sherry
3 tablespoons cornstarch, divided
½ cup cold water
3½ cups chicken broth
¼ teaspoon salt
1 tablespoon soy sauce
¼ cup thinly sliced mushrooms
¼ cup canned bamboo shoots, cut into thin strips
½ cup bean curd, shredded
1 egg, slightly beaten
2 tablespoons cider vinegar
3 to 4 drops hot red pepper sauce
1 tablespoon sesame oil
1 tablespoon minced scallion

In a small bowl, stir together pork, sherry and 1 teaspoon cornstarch. Mix remaining cornstarch with cold water in another bowl.

Pour chicken broth into large saucepan. Add salt and soy sauce. Bring to a boil, stir in pork mixture and cook for 1 minute. Add mushrooms, bamboo shoots and bean curd, cooking for another minute. Then stir in well-stirred cornstarch and water mixture. Continue stirring as soup thickens. While stirring, mix in egg. Add vinegar, pepper sauce and oil. Cook and stir until thoroughly mixed or about 1 minute. Serve garnished with scallion.

Makes 6 servings.

Stir-Fry Chicken and Pea Pods

Be sure to have all ingredients prepared before you begin cooking.

2 teaspooons water
1 teaspoon cornstarch
½ teaspooon sugar
2 teaspoons sesame oil
4 drops hot red pepper sauce
2 teaspoons red wine vinegar
2 tablespoons chicken broth
2 teaspoons soy sauce
3 tablespoons vegetable oil
1 garlic clove, minced
1 teaspoon grated fresh ginger
2 cups boneless chicken meat, cut into thin strips
½ cup chopped green onion
½ lb. pea pods, stringed and cut diagonally

In a small bowl, stir together water and cornstarch. In another small bowl, stir together sugar, sesame oil, pepper sauce, vinegar, chicken broth and soy sauce. In a wok or fry pan over high heat, cook together oil, garlic and ginger for ½ minute. Stir in chicken meat and cook for about 3 to 5 minutes or until chicken meat is cooked; remove from pan. Add green onion and pea pods to wok. Cook, stirring continuously until tender, about 3 to 5 minutes. Return chicken meat mixture to wok. Pour in sugar-chicken broth mixture, let come to boil. Pour in cornstarch mixture and stir until sauce thickens. Stir several more times and serve.

Makes 4 servings.

MENU

Hot and Sour Soup

Stir-Fry Chicken and Pea Pods

Fluffy White Rice

Stir-Fry Bean Sprouts

Fresh Pineapple Chunks

Fluffy White Rice

If you prefer drier rice, reduce water by ¼ cup; or add ¼ cup water to recipe if you like moister rice.

2 cups water
1 tablespoon butter or margarine
1 teaspoon salt
1 cup long grain rice

In a saucepan, bring water, butter and salt to boil over moderate heat. Stir in rice. Cover and lower heat to simmer. Cook for 20 minutes. Fluff and serve.

Makes 6 servings.

Stir-Fry Bean Sprouts

The secret in this dish is the short cooking time, so have all ingredients ready before you begin.

½ teaspoon grated fresh ginger
1 tablespoon thin soy sauce
2 teaspoons sesame oil
2 to 3 drops hot red pepper sauce
½ teaspoon salt
3 tablespoons vegetable oil
4 cups fresh bean sprouts

In a small bowl, stir together ginger, soy sauce, sesame oil, pepper sauce, and salt. Set aside.

Pour oil into fry pan over moderately high heat. When oil is hot, add bean sprouts and stir-fry for ½ minute. Stir in ginger-soy mixture. Stir-fry an additional ½ minute.

Makes 4 servings.

Fresh Pineapple Chunks

This dessert makes wonderful use of an electric knife.

1 ripe, fresh pineapple
3 tablespoons powdered sugar

Cut off top and bottom of pineapple. Stand pineapple on one end and cut off rind. Quarter pineapple and remove core from each quarter. Cut pineapple into chunks and place in a bowl. Sprinkle with powdered sugar and refrigerate until thoroughly chilled.

Makes about 4 servings.

MENU

Hot and Sour Soup

Stir-Fry Chicken and Pea Pods

Fluffy White Rice

Stir-Fry Bean Sprouts

Fresh Pineapple Chunks

Savory Glazed Corned Beef

Remember to check the amount of water in the pot periodically as the corned beef simmers.

1 (3 lb.) corned beef brisket
¼ cup ketchup
1 tablespoon butter or margarine
1½ tablespoons red wine vinegar
1 tablespoon prepared mustard
3 tablespoons brown sugar

Place corned beef brisket in a large saucepan and add enough water to cover. Bring to a boil over high heat. Reduce heat to simmer and cook for 3 to 3½ hours or until meat is fork-tender; drain.

Meanwhile, place ketchup, butter, vinegar, mustard and brown sugar in a small saucepan. Bring to a boil over high heat; remove from heat and set aside.

Place boiled corned beef on a rack in a shallow open roasting pan. Spoon the glaze over meat. Roast at 350° F. for 20 minutes, basting occasionally with additional glaze.

Makes 6 to 8 servings.

Steamed Cabbage Wedges

A natural with corned beef.

1 medium green cabbage
1 teaspoon caraway seeds

Remove any outer wilted leaves and cut cabbage head into 6 to 8 wedges. Trim hardest portion of core.

Cook cabbage in salted boiling water until tender. Drain. Sprinkle with caraway seeds.

Makes 6 servings.

Lemon Buttered Turnips

Turnips also are delicious eaten raw.

1 lb. turnips, peeled and sliced
1 teaspoon lemon juice
2 tablespoons butter or margarine, melted
¼ teaspoon salt

In a saucepan, cook turnips in rapidly boiling salted water until tender; drain. Add lemon juice, butter and salt. Toss gently to coat turnip slices with lemon butter.

Makes 4 servings.

Mixed Green Salad

Walnuts add a special taste and texture to the salad.

¼ head iceberg lettuce
1 cup spinach, washed and trimmed
½ cucumber, peeled and thinly sliced
¼ cup broken walnut pieces

Into a large bowl, tear greens into bite-size pieces. Add cucumber and walnuts. Top with ⅓ cup of your favorite dressing. Toss and serve.

Makes 4 servings.

MENU

Savory Glazed Corned Beef

Steamed Cabbage Wedges

Lemon Buttered Turnips

Mixed Green Salad

Irish Coffee Mousse

Irish Coffee Mousse

Just as delicious after a meal as drinking Irish coffee.

1 envelope (1 tablespoon) unflavored gelatin
3 tablespoons cold water
¾ cup strong, hot coffee
4 tablespoons sugar
1½ tablespoons Irish whiskey
1 cup heavy cream
2 tablespoon's powdered sugar
¼ cup grated semi-sweet chocolate

In a bowl, soak gelatin in cold water for 5 minutes. Stir in coffee until gelatin is dissolved. Add sugar and whiskey, stirring until sugar dissolves. Chill until mixture mounds easily with a spoon. Meanwhile, whip cream with powdered sugar until stiff. Fold heavy cream into coffee-gelatin mixture. Spoon into individual serving dishes. Sprinkle with chocolate. Chill until set.

Makes 4 servings.

Asparagus Vinaigrette

This is delicious as a first course or as a salad.

2 lbs. fresh asparagus
2 tablespoons wine vinegar
½ teaspoon Dijon mustard
⅛ teaspoon salt
dash ground pepper
½ cup olive oil
1 tablespoon capers
1 tablespoon chopped pimiento
lettuce leaves, cleaned and crisped

Cook asparagus in rapidly boiling salted water until tender; drain and chill.

In a bowl, beat together vinegar, mustard, salt and pepper. Then, slowly beat in oil. Stir in capers and chopped pimiento.

Arrange asparagus on lettuce leaves. Spoon dressing over asparagus.

Makes 4 servings.

Roast Rib of Beef

Standing rib roast is truly the most elegant of roast beefs.

1   2 to 3 rib standing rib of beef roast (about 6 to 8 lbs.)

Place roast, fat side up, on rib bones in open roasting pan. Place in 325° F. oven and roast, uncovered, according to timetable below:

Weight of Roast (pounds)	Hours to Reach Desired Doneness		
	Rare	Medium	Well-Done
4	2	2½	2¾
6	2½	3	3½
8	3	3½	4¼
10	4½	5	5¼

Meat has reached desired degree of doneness when internal temperature is: 140° F. for rare; 160° F. for medium; 170° F. for well-done. Let meat rest for at least 15 minutes before carving.

Makes 12 to 16 servings.

Duchess Potatoes

These potatoes may be shaped into individual servings or used as a border for casseroles or planked meats.

4 medium potatoes
½ teaspoon salt
dash ground pepper
1 egg yolk, slightly beaten
3 tablespoons butter or margarine, melted
paprika

Peel potatoes and cut into large pieces. Cook in salted boiling water for about 20 minutes or until tender; drain. In a large bowl, mash potatoes with salt and pepper until very smooth. Stir in egg yolk. Using a pastry bag with fluted tube, pipe potatoes into four large rosettes on a greased baking sheet. Or, using a spoon, simply make 4 mounds of potato on a baking sheet. Drizzle potatoes with butter and sprinkle with paprika. Bake at 400° F. for about 15 minutes or until golden brown.

Makes 4 servings.

Sautéed Peas and Onions

As a variation on this recipe, substitute mushroom slices for onion and add a bit of lemon juice.

4 tablespoons butter or margarine
⅓ cup chopped onion
3½ lbs. fresh green peas, shelled (or 2 (10 oz.) packages frozen peas)
¼ teaspoon ground pepper

In a fry pan, melt butter. Add onion and cook over moderate heat until onions are translucent. Stir in peas and pepper and continue cooking for about 5 to 8 minutes or until peas are tender.

Makes 6 servings.

Strawberry Sour Cream Gelatin Mold

This salad is good enough to become dessert, if you wish.

1 package (3 oz.) mixed fruit flavor gelatin
1 cup boiling water
1 cup sour cream
1 pint fresh strawberries, hulled and halved
1 cup seedless grapes
salad greens

Place gelatin in a bowl. Stir in boiling water until dissolved. Beat in sour cream until well mixed. Stir in strawberries and grapes. Pour into individual molds or a single 5-cup mold. Chill until set. Unmold onto salad greens.

Makes 4 servings.

Mocha Ice Cream Roll

This is a wonderful make-ahead dessert.

4 eggs, separated
½ cup powdered sugar
1 teaspoon vanilla extract
4 tablespoons cocoa
1 quart coffee ice cream, softened
1 pint hot fudge sauce, warmed

Grease a 15½″ x 10½″ jelly-roll pan. Line with baking parchment; grease and flour paper.

In a small bowl, beat together egg yolks with powdered sugar until creamy. Stir in vanilla and cocoa. Set aside. In a large bowl, beat egg whites until soft peaks form. Beating at high speed, add powdered sugar. Continue beating until sugar is completely dissolved. Gently fold egg yolk mixture into beaten whites with rubber spatula. Spread batter evenly in pan. Bake at 400° F. for 15 minutes or until top springs back when lightly touched with finger. Sprinkle a clean cloth towel with powdered sugar.

When cake is done, immediately turn out onto the towel. Remove paper, and roll up jelly-roll fashion from narrow end. Cool. When cake is cool, unroll and spread with ice cream. Re-roll, wrap well and place in freezer, seam side down. Freeze. Slice and serve with hot fudge sauce.

Makes 10 servings.

Roast Capon with Lemon-Tarragon Sauce

A slightly tart, savory sauce enhances a simple roast capon.

1 (6 to 8 lb.) capon, rinsed and drained well
1 cup chicken broth
1 teaspoon dried tarragon leaves
2 teaspoons lemon juice
¼ teaspoon Kitchen Bouquet
¼ teaspoon salt
dash ground pepper
1 tablespoon cornstarch
2 tablespoons dry white wine or dry vermouth

Fold wings up and under back of capon. With string, tie legs and tail together. Place capon, breast side up, on a rack in an open roasting pan. Roast at 325° F. for about 3½ hours or until internal temperature reaches 180° to 185° F.

Meanwhile, in a saucepan, stir together chicken broth, tarragon, lemon juice, Kitchen Bouquet, salt and pepper. In a small bowl, stir together cornstarch and wine.

When capon is cooked, remove it from the pan and pour drippings into another small bowl. Keep capon warm while preparing sauce. Skim fat off of top of drippings. Strain drippings into saucepan with chicken broth. Place the sauce pan over moderate heat and cook until mixture comes to boil. Reduce heat and simmer for 3 to 5 minutes. Stir in corn starch mixture and cook until sauce thickens. Carve capon and serve with sauce.

Makes 8 servings.

Noodle Pudding

Serve noodle pudding hot or warm with sour cream as a garnish.

6 oz. egg noodles
2 eggs, slightly beaten
4 tablespoons sugar
½ teaspoon ground cinnamon
3 tablespoons butter or margarine, melted and cooled
½ pint (8 oz.) cottage cheese
¼ cup sour cream
¼ cup raisins

In a saucepan, cook noodles according to package directions; drain and cool. Meanwhile, in a large bowl, stir together eggs, sugar, cinnamon, butter, cottage cheese, sour cream and raisins. Stir in cooked noodles. Spoon noodle mixture into a buttered 1½ quart casserole. Bake at 350° F., uncovered, for 1 hour.

Makes 4 to 6 servings.

Creamed Spinach

Nutmeg is the key to the flavor of this vegetable recipe.

1 package (10 oz.) fresh spinach
3 tablespoons butter or margarine
3 tablespoons flour
¾ cup milk
½ teaspoon salt
⅛ teaspoon ground pepper
¼ teaspoon ground nutmeg

In large saucepan, cook spinach over moderate heat until wilted; drain. Chop spinach.

In another saucepan, melt butter over moderate heat. Add flour and cook for 5 minutes, stirring occasionally without browning flour. Beat in milk and cook sauce until it comes to a boil, stirring continuously. Stir in salt, pepper and nutmeg. Add chopped spinach and again bring to a boil while stirring.

Makes 4 servings.

Corn Relish

Use first-of-the-season fresh corn and lay in a supply of this delicious relish. With an electric knife, the preparation is easy.

**6 cups fresh corn kernels (cut from about 12 ears)
3 cups finely chopped onion
1½ cups finely diced green pepper
1⅓ cups finely diced red pepper
1 cup sugar
2 cups cider vinegar
2 teaspoons salt
1 teaspoon dry mustard
½ teaspoon celery seed
½ teaspoon turmeric
¼ teaspoon cayenne pepper**

Combine all the ingredients in a heavy saucepan. Bring to a boil and simmer, stirring for 10 minutes. Spoon into sterilized one-pint canning jars, allowing ½-inch headroom. Process in a boiling water bath for 15 minutes. Complete seals. Cool and store in a cupboard for at least a week before using.

Makes 4 pints.

Fresh Fruit Tarts

Prepare tarts with a selection of fruits of the season. Make some tarts strawberry, some peach or . . . .

**4 cups cut up fresh fruit
6 baked tart shells
1 cup currant jelly
1 tablespoon water
1 tablespoon kirsch
⅓ cup whipped heavy cream**

Arrange fruit in tart shells. In a saucepan, dissolve currant jelly with water over moderately high heat. Remove from heat; stir in kirsch. Cool briefly. Spoon currant jelly mixture over top of fruit as a glaze. Garnish top of each tart with a dollop of whipped cream.

Makes 6 servings.

Crumb Baked Fish

If fresh fish is available, you may want to purchase whole fish and make your own fillets.

½ cup fine, dry bread crumbs
¼ teaspoon salt
⅛ teaspoon ground pepper
⅛ teaspoon paprika
¼ teaspoon fennel seed
1 lb. flounder or sole fillets
2 tablespoons oil
3 tablespoons lemon juice

In a shallow bowl, stir together crumbs, salt, pepper, paprika and fennel. Brush both sides of fish with oil. Dip fish in crumbs and place on a baking sheet. Sprinkle with lemon juice. Bake at 400° F. for 10 to 15 minutes or just until fish flakes easily with a fork.

Makes 4 servings.

Baked Onions Au Gratin

This recipe may be prepared early in the day and refrigerated. Then just add 10 minutes to the cooking time when you bake it before serving.

4 tablespoons butter or margarine
4 tablespoons flour
1½ cups milk
½ teaspoon salt
⅛ teaspoon ground pepper
2 cups shredded Cheddar cheese, divided
2 jars (16 oz.) whole, small boiled onions, drained
paprika

In a saucepan, melt butter over moderate heat. Stir in flour and cook for 5 minutes without browning flour. Beat in milk, salt and pepper; cook until thickened, stirring continuously. Stir in 1½ cups cheese and cook until cheese is melted. Remove from heat and stir in onions. Pour into 1½ quart casserole. Sprinkle top with remaining cheese and then paprika. Bake at 350° F., uncovered, for 20 minutes.

Makes 4 to 6 servings.

MENU

Crumb Baked Fish
Baked Onions Au Gratin
Pan Fried Zucchini
Melon with Lime
Fudge-Topped Petit Fours

Pan Fried Zucchini

Any summer squash may be used in this recipe — crookneck, patty pan or zucchini.

1 garlic clove, minced
3 tablespoons vegetable oil
4 medium zucchini, cut into ¼-inch thick slices
1 teaspoon dried leaf oregano
½ teaspoon salt
⅛ teaspoon ground pepper

In a fry pan, sauté garlic in oil over moderate heat for 2 to 3 minutes. Add zucchini, oregano, salt and pepper. Cook for 8 to 10 minutes, stirring occasionally, until zucchini is tender.

Makes 4 servings.

Melon with Lime

The electric knife is superb at making melon wedges, slices and chunks. Select your favorite **ripe melon** and serve it chilled with a **wedge of lime or lemon.**

Fudge-Topped Petit Fours

The electric knife makes cutting these little cakes a very simple task.

1 package (18.5 oz.) yellow cake mix or chocolate cake mix
2 eggs
3 cups sugar
1 cup milk
3 tablespoons light corn syrup
3 squares unsweetened chocolate
⅓ cup butter or margarine, cut into small pieces
1 teaspoon vanilla extract

Prepare cake batter according to package directions, using eggs. Pour into greased and floured 9″ x 13″ pan. Bake according to package directions; cool.

Meanwhile in a saucepan, stir together sugar, milk, corn syrup and chocolate. Place over moderate heat and bring to a boil, stirring occasionally until sugar is dissolved and chocolate melted. Set candy thermometer in place and continue cooking, stirring occasionally, until temperature reaches 232° F. Remove from heat immediately and add butter.

Cool mixture without stirring until temperature reaches 110° F. Meanwhile cut cake into 32 squares and place squares on a rack over baking sheet. When chocolate reaches temperature, add vanilla and beat for 3 to 5 minutes until mixture thickens a bit, but not too long. Quickly pour fudge over top of cake squares, letting some fudge run down edges of cake unevenly. Allow fudge to set before serving. If desired, garnish with a rosette of whipped cream at time of serving.

Makes 32 petit fours.

MENU

Crumb Baked Fish

Baked Onions Au Gratin

Pan Fried Zucchini

Melon with Lime

Fudge-Topped Petit Fours

Roast Pork Tenderloin

Tart-sweet currant glaze gives pork roast a succulent flavor.

½ cup red currant jelly
¼ teaspoon grated orange rind
1 tablespoon orange juice
2 pork tenderloins (about 1 lb. each)

In a small saucepan over moderate heat, stir together jelly, orange rind and orange juice. Bring to a boil and stir until jelly is dissolved. Remove glaze from heat; set aside.

Place tenderloins on a rack in an open roasting pan. Baste with glaze. Roast at 325° F. for 1 hour or until meat thermometer reaches 170° F., basting periodically with glaze. Carve meat into thin slices.

Makes 6 to 8 servings.

Whole Artichokes with Hollandaise Sauce

Whole artichokes are elegant as a vegetable or as a first course. If you wish, serve with a simple lemon butter or vinaigrette dressing.

4 large whole artichokes
3 egg yolks
1 tablespoon lemon juice
1 tablespoon water
¼ teaspoon salt
dash ground pepper
¼ lb. (1 stick) butter, melted and warm

Trim ends of artichoke leaves and cut off stems. Place in a large pot of rapidly boiling salted water. Cover pot and cook for about 30 minutes or until stem end pierces readily with a fork. Meanwhile, prepare hollandaise sauce.

Hollandaise Sauce:

Place egg yolks in top of double boiler. Beat in lemon juice, water, salt and pepper. Set top of double boiler over simmering water. Stir continuously until egg barely begins to thicken. Immediately remove from heat and beat in butter, ¼ teaspoon at a time at first and then in a very slow steady stream until all butter is incorporated. Serve warm.

Makes 4 servings.

Skillet Mushrooms

Plan on these mushrooms in smaller quantity as a garnish to top steaks and chops.

1 lb. fresh mushrooms, cleaned and halved
6 tablespoons butter or margarine
1 tablespoon lemon juice
½ teaspoon salt
⅛ teaspoon ground pepper
2 teaspoons minced parsley

Place mushrooms in a fry pan with butter over moderate heat. Add lemon juice, salt and pepper. Sauté for about 5 minutes or until mushrooms are tender. Sprinkle with parsley.

Makes 4 servings.

Marinated Cucumbers and Tomatoes

Here's a refreshing salad with a zesty peppery taste.

2 medium cucumbers
12 cherry tomatoes
1 teaspoon soy sauce
2 tablespoons cider vinegar
2 tablespoons sugar
1½ tablespoons vegetable oil
¼ teaspoon hot red pepper sauce
1 teaspoon salt
4 crisp lettuce leaves

Peel, halve and seed cucumbers. Cut crosswise into ½-inch chunks and place in a bowl. Halve cherry tomatoes and add to cucumbers; set aside.

In another bowl, stir together soy sauce, vinegar, sugar, oil, pepper sauce and salt. Pour soy mixture over tomatoes and cucumbers. Toss and chill. Serve on lettuce leaves.

Makes 4 servings.

Chocolate Chip Cheesecake

Chocolate bits are a delicious twist in this rich cheesecake.

1 cup crushed graham cracker crumbs
1⅛ cups sugar, divided
¼ cup butter or margarine, melted
12 ounces cream cheese, softened
2 eggs, separated
1 teaspoon vanilla extract
1 package (6 oz.) semi-sweet chocolate bits
1 cup sour cream

In a bowl, stir together graham cracker crumbs, ¼ cup sugar and melted butter. Press mixture into bottom of 9-inch springform pan. Set aside.

In another bowl, beat cream cheese with ¾ cup sugar until creamy. Add egg yolks and vanilla; mix well. Add chocolate bits and stir. In a small bowl, beat egg whites until stiff. Fold whites into cream cheese mixture. Pour into crust-lined pan and bake at 350° F. for 30 minutes. Meanwhile, stir together sour cream with remaining 2 tablespoons sugar in a bowl.

Remove cake from the oven. Spread top with sour cream mixture. Return cake to oven for an additional 5 minutes. Chill and serve.

Makes 1 (9-inch) cheesecake.

MENU

Roast Pork Tenderloin

Whole Artichokes with Hollandaise Sauce

Skillet Mushrooms

Marinated Cucumbers and Tomatoes

Chocolate Chip Cheesecake

Pasta è Fagioli

The name means simply pasta with beans — a hearty Italian soup.

1 cup dry white beans
1 small onion, chopped
⅓ cup chopped celery
2 garlic cloves, minced
3 tablespoons olive oil
½ lb. smoked ham, cut in small cubes
¼ lb. salt pork
1½ teaspoons salt
¼ teaspoon ground pepper
1 tablespoon tomato paste
½ cup pasta (spaghetti, small shells or small macaroni)
grated Parmesan cheese

In pot or bowl, soak beans overnight in enough water to cover. Drain beans, reserving liquid. In another saucepan, sauté onion, celery and garlic in oil until onions are tender. Stir in ham, and continue cooking for 3 to 5 minutes. Add beans, salt, pepper, and tomato paste and reserved liquid plus enough water to make 8 cups. Bring soup to boil and reduce heat to simmer for 1½ hours or until beans are tender. Remove half of the beans, purée and return to soup. Add pasta and simmer for 15 to 20 minutes. Taste for seasoning. Serve with grated Parmesan cheese.

Makes 6 to 8 servings.

French Bread Pizza

Try this marvelous way to have homemade pizza without the fuss of making a crust.

1 loaf French bread
1 cup canned Italian tomatoes
2 garlic cloves, peeled
1 small onion, peeled
¼ teaspoon salt
1 teaspoon dried leaf oregano
½ teaspoon dried basil leaves
⅛ teaspoon crushed red pepper
4 tablespoons vegetable oil
4 ounces thinly sliced pepperoni
2 cups grated mozzarella cheese

Slice bread in half horizontally and then in half again cross-wise. Place bread on baking sheet and broil until bread is golden brown. In the container of a blender or food processor, purée tomatoes, garlic, onion, salt, oregano, basil and red pepper; set aside.

Brush toasted bread pieces with 1 tablespoon oil each. Spoon tomato sauce onto bread. Arrange pepperoni over tomato sauce and top with cheese. Bake at 450° F. for 5 to 10 minutes, until cheese is melted and browned.

Makes 4 servings.

MENU

Pasta è Fagioli

French Bread Pizza

Almond Honey Ice Cream

Meringue Chocolate Chip Cookies

Almond Honey Ice Cream

Enjoy the fun of homemade ice cream without an ice cream freezer.

6 egg yolks
1 cup honey
2 cups light cream
¼ teaspoon almond extract
½ cup coarsely chopped almonds

In the top of a double boiler, stir together egg yolks and honey. Cook until mixture thickens slightly. Remove from heat; cool to room temperature. Stir in cream, almond extract and almonds. Pour into a shallow container. Place in the freezer. When mixture is frozen around the edges and soft in the center, stir. Cover and allow to freeze firmly.

Makes 6 servings.

Meringue Chocolate Chip Cookies

Here's a delicately light cookie that can be a special treat when there are extra egg whites in the house.

3 egg whites
1 cup sugar
1 teaspoon vanilla extract
1 cup semi-sweet chocolate bits

In a bowl, beat egg whites with rotary beater until soft peaks form. Slowly add sugar, beating until egg whites hold stiff peaks and sugar is dissolved. Beat in vanilla. Stir in chocolate bits. Spoon batter, by the tablespoon, onto a baking sheet covered with brown paper. Bake at 300° F. for 25 to 30 minutes.

Makes about 2 dozen cookies.

Summer

Italian Antipasto Platter

Enjoy this light supper for a hot summer's eve.

Antipasto:

1 head lettuce, washed and crisped
3 tomatoes, cut into wedges
1 cucumber, peeled and sliced
8 slices Genoa salami
8 slices prosciutto or mortadella
4 slices provolone cheese, halved
1 can (6½ or 7 oz.) tuna, drained
1 can (3¾ oz.) sardines in oil, drained
1 can (2 oz.) rolled anchovy fillets, drained
8 radishes
8 ripe olives
2 cups Caponata

Dressing:

¼ cup lemon juice
1 garlic clove, minced
¼ teaspoon salt
dash ground pepper
½ teaspoon dried basil leaves
½ cup olive oil

Line serving platter with outside leaves of lettuce. Tear remaining lettuce into bite-size pieces and place on platter. Arrange remaining antipasto ingredients on top of lettuce. Cover and chill thoroughly.

Meanwhile, in a small bowl, stir together lemon juice, garlic, salt, pepper, basil and olive oil for dressing. Pour dressing over antipasto and serve.

Makes 4 servings.

MENU
Italian Antipasto Platter
Caponata
Garlic Bread
Almond Macaroons
Summer Sangria

Caponata

This is a flavorful cold relish made of chopped eggplant, celery, onion and tomato. It can be prepared up to 4 days before serving.

½ lb. eggplant, peeled and cut into ½-inch cubes
1 tablespoon salt
3 tablespoons vegetable oil, divided
½ cup chopped celery
½ cup chopped onion
1½ tablespoons red wine vinegar
1½ teaspoons sugar
8 oz. canned whole tomatoes, drained and chopped
2 tablespoons chopped green olives
⅛ teaspoon ground black pepper

In a colander, sprinkle eggplant with salt. Set aside to drain for 30 minutes.

In a large skillet, heat 1½ tablespoons oil over medium heat. Add chopped celery and onion and cook 15 minutes, stirring frequently. Remove from pan; add remaining oil and drained eggplant; cook stirring continuously for 5 minutes until lightly browned. Add celery mixture, vinegar, sugar, tomatoes, olives and pepper. Simmer mixture uncovered, stirring frequently, for 15 minutes. Remove from heat; refrigerate. Serve chilled.

Makes 2 cups.

Garlic Bread

The traditional favorite for Italian meals is easy to make ahead and heat just before serving.

1 loaf French or Italian bread
½ cup butter or margarine
1 garlic clove, minced
1 tablespoon chopped parsley

Cut French bread into slices almost through bottom of loaf; set aside. In a small saucepan, over moderate heat, melt butter. Add garlic and parsley. Cook for 3 minutes and remove from heat. Brush cut surfaces of bread with garlic butter. Bake loaf for 15 to 20 minutes at 375° F.

Makes 1 loaf garlic bread.

Almond Macaroons

Cookie tops may be sprinkled with pine nuts, sliced almonds or left plain.

1 pound almond paste
2 cups sugar
4 tablespoons flour
⅔ cup sifted powdered sugar
⅔ cup egg whites (about 6 whites), unbeaten
1 cup pine nuts

In a bowl, soften almond paste by hand. Work in sugar, salt, flour, powdered sugar and egg whites. Line baking sheet with brown paper. Drop batter, 1 teaspoon at a time, 2 inches apart on paper. Gently press some pine nuts into the tops of cookies. Bake at 325° F. for about 20 minutes or until lightly browned.

Makes about 5 dozen cookies.

Summer Sangria

A wonderful refresher for a warm summer dinner.

1 bottle red wine
2 oz. Triple Sec or Cointreau
2 limes, sliced
1 lemon, sliced
2 oranges, sliced
1 tablespoon sugar
ice

Pour wine and Triple Sec into pitcher. Squeeze limes, lemons and oranges into wine and put fruit into pitcher. Add sugar and stir. Add ice cubes and stir again.

Makes 4 to 6 servings.

Gazpacho Soup

Refrigerating this soup for several hours before serving allows the flavors to fully develop and blend.

3 medium tomatoes, peeled, seeded and quartered
1 medium green pepper, seeded and quartered
1 medium onion, peeled and quartered
1 garlic clove, peeled
3 tablespoons lemon juice
¾ teaspoon salt
3 drops hot red pepper sauce
1 cup tomato juice
seasoned croutons

Purée the tomatoes, green pepper, onion and garlic clove in the container of a blender or food processor. Transfer the mixture to a large bowl or pitcher. Stir in lemon juice, salt, pepper sauce and tomato juice. Refrigerate for at least 6 hours before serving.

Stir and serve with crouton garnish.

Makes 4 servings.

Sunny Barbecued Ribs

Lemonade concentrate gives this barbecue sauce a fresh tang.

1¼ cups ketchup
1 can (6 oz.) frozen lemonade concentrate, thawed
¾ cup water
2 tablespoons Worcestershire sauce
¼ cup prepared mustard
2 tablespoons vegetable oil
2 tablespoons instant minced onion
4 lbs. pork country ribs or back ribs, cut into serving pieces

In a saucepan, stir together ketchup, lemonade concentrate, water, Worcestershire sauce, mustard, oil and onion. Heat to boiling and simmer for 10 minutes. Set aside.

Place ribs on grill over hot coals; grill for 10 minutes, turning once. Brush generously with barbecue sauce mixture and continue cooking for another 20 minutes or until fork-tender, turning often and basting.

Makes 4 servings.

Potatoes in Foil

Enjoy these potatoes with the skin still on, or peel them if you wish.

4 tablespoons butter or margarine
4 medium potatoes, well-scrubbed and thinly sliced
1 small onion, very thinly sliced
½ teaspoon salt
⅛ teaspoon ground pepper

Arrange 2 strips of aluminum foil to make a pouch for potatoes. Butter foil, using 1 tablespoon butter. Arrange a layer of potatoes on buttered foil, using ¼ of the potatoes. Top with a layer of ¼ the onion, then some salt and pepper. Repeat layers 3 more times. Seal foil well around potatoes. Place on the grill over hot coals. Cook for 20 minutes. Turn over and cook for an additional 20 minutes.

Makes 4 servings.

Colorful Cole Slaw

This is a bright slaw made with radishes and green pepper.

4 cups shredded cabbage
1 small green pepper, seeded and thinly sliced
½ cup sliced radishes
2 tablespoons grated onion
1 cup mayonnaise
2 tablespoons cider vinegar
2 tablespoons light cream
1 teaspoon salt
½ teaspoon sugar
¼ teaspoon ground pepper

In a bowl, toss together cabbage, pepper, radishes and onion. In another bowl, stir together mayonnaise, vinegar, cream, salt, sugar, and pepper. Pour mayonnaise mixture over cabbage mixture and toss gently. Cover and refrigerate.

Makes 4 servings.

MENU
Gazpacho Soup
Sunny Barbecued Ribs
Potatoes in Foil
Colorful Cole Slaw
Peach Shortcake

Peach Shortcake

A touch of almond extract heightens the fresh peach flavor.

3 cups sliced fresh peaches
⅛ teaspoon almond extract
6 tablespoons sugar
2 cups flour
1 tablespoon baking powder
½ teaspoon salt
4 tablespoons butter or margarine
¾ cup milk
1 cup heavy cream, whipped
3 tablespoons sliced almonds

In a bowl, stir together peaches, almond extract and 4 tablespoons sugar; set aside.

Sift together into a bowl, flour, 2 tablespoons sugar, baking powder and salt. Cut in butter until mixture resembles coarse crumbs. Stir in milk all at once. Turn dough out onto floured surface; knead gently for ½ minute. Pat or roll to ½-inch thickness. Cut six 2½-inch biscuits from dough. Place biscuits on baking sheet and bake at 450° F. for about 10 minutes or until golden brown. Cool and split biscuits.

To serve, place biscuit bottom on serving plate. Top with peach slices, top of biscuit, whipped cream and garnish with almond slices.

Makes 6 servings.

Frosty Cucumber Soup

Try serving garnished with a dollop of sour cream and dash of dill.

4 medium cucumbers, peeled, halved and seeded
1 medium onion, peeled and chopped
4 tablespoons butter or margarine
2 cups chicken broth
1 cup light cream
½ teaspoon salt
⅛ teaspoon ground pepper

Place cucumbers, onion and butter in a saucepan over moderate heat. Cover and cook until onions are transparent and cucumbers are tender. Place these ingredients in the container of a blender or food processor and purée. Pour into bowl and stir in broth, cream, salt and pepper. Chill well.

Makes 4 servings.

Flank Steak Teriyaki

Carving the meat cross grain gives you more tender eating.

2½ cups unsweetened pineapple juice
⅓ cup soy sauce
1 (1½ to 2 lb.) flank steak

In large shallow pan, stir together pineapple juice and soy sauce to make marinade. Add flank steak and refrigerate for 1 day, turning once. Remove steak from marinade and cook on a grill over hot coals or broil to desired degree of doneness. To carve, cut across the grain of the meat.

Makes 4 servings.

MENU

Frosty Cucumber Soup
Flank Steak Teriyaki
Corn on the Cob
Grilled Onion Slices
Garden Salad
Mustard French Dressing
Festive Melon Boat

Corn on the Cob

Sugar in the cooking water gives fresh corn that wonderful hint of sweetness.

4 ears corn on the cob
2 tablespoons sugar

Remove husks and silks from corn. Place corn in large pot of boiling water to which sugar has been added. Cover and cook for 3 to 5 minutes. Drain.

Makes 4 servings.

Grilled Onion Slices

A hearty accompaniment for summer cook-outs.

2 large Bermuda onions, peeled

Cut onions into ½-inch thick slices. Place on grill over hot coals. Cook for 10 minutes on one side; turn and cook an additional 10 minutes.

Makes 4 servings.

Garden Salad

Here's a salad that can be made by harvesting the most common homegrown vegetables.

1 medium zucchini, washed and sliced
2 tomatoes, sliced
2 medium green peppers, seeded and sliced
¼ cup chopped chives
lettuce leaves, washed and crisped

Arrange zucchini, tomato and green pepper on lettuce leaves. Sprinkle with chopped chives. Serve with Mustard French Dressing.

Makes 4 servings.

Mustard French Dressing

This is a simple variation on classic French dressing.

½ cup vegetable oil
¼ cup lemon juice
1 tablespoon prepared mustard
½ teaspoon salt
¼ teaspoon ground pepper
½ teaspoon dried leaf oregano
dash garlic powder

In a small covered jar, shake together oil, lemon juice, mustard, salt, pepper, oregano and garlic powder. Allow to stand for 1 hour. Pour over salad greens to serve.

Makes ¾ cup dressing.

Festive Melon Boat

Plan this beautiful fruit boat as the centerpiece for a party.

1 long, medium-size watermelon

Using an electric knife, slice about ¼ from top of melon. Make another thin slice at opposite side of melon just to remove rind and give melon boat a solid resting surface. Scoop out fruit from both top and bottom sections of melon, leaving a thick rind. With knife, cut even sawtooth pattern around top of shell. Cube melon or make melon balls and return fruit to shell. If desired, add other cut up melons or additional fruits to melon boat. Cover and chill thoroughly.

MENU

Frosty Cucumber Soup

Flank Steak Teriyaki

Corn on the Cob

Grilled Onion Slices

Garden Salad

Mustard French Dressing

Festive Melon Boat

Herb Grilled Fish

Choose your favorite fish for this recipe — salmon, cod, sword-fish . . .

½ **cup butter or margarine**
2 **teaspoons lemon juice**
½ **teaspoon dill weed**
½ **teaspoon dried rosemary leaves**
½ **teaspoon Summer Savory**
⅛ **teaspoon ground black pepper**
4 **(6 oz. each) fish steaks**

In a small saucepan, melt butter. Stir in lemon juice, dill, rosemary, Summer Savory and pepper. Cook fish steaks over hot coals, basting frequently with butter mixture. Turn and baste on other side until fish is cooked.

Makes 4 servings.

Rice Noodle Pilaf

To vary the flavor of this pilaf, you may want to substitute beef broth for chicken broth.

6 **tablespoons butter or margarine**
1 **small onion, peeled and chopped**
1 **cup long grain rice**
1 **cup fine noodles, broken into 2-inch pieces**
2 **cups chicken broth**

Melt butter in a saucepan over moderate heat. Add onions and cook until tender. Add rice and noodles, cooking until noodles turn golden brown. Pour in chicken broth, cover and cook over low heat for about 20 minutes or until all liquid is absorbed. Fluff and serve.

Makes 6 servings.

Vegetables on the Grill

A simple addition to the outdoor chef's repertoire.

2 medium summer squash, sliced
1 medium green pepper, seeded and thinly sliced
2 tomatoes, chopped
1 tablespoon vegetable oil
aluminum foil
1 teaspoon salt
¼ teaspoon ground pepper
1 teaspoon dried sweet basil leaves
2 tablespoons butter or margarine

Place half of the summer squash, green pepper and tomato in the center of a piece of oiled aluminum foil. Sprinkle with half of the salt, pepper, and basil. Repeat layers and dot top with butter. Fold foil around vegetables and seal edges well.

Cook vegetables in foil pouch over hot coals for 15 minutes. Turn pouch over and cook an additional 10 minutes.

Makes 4 servings.

Strawberries Smetane

A simple topping to prepare and a favorite on strawberries, blueberries or peaches.

1¼ cups sour cream
¼ cup brown sugar
1 quart fresh strawberries, washed and hulled

In a bowl, stir together sour cream and brown sugar until sugar is dissolved. Spoon strawberries into individual serving dishes. Top with sour cream mixture.

Makes 6 servings.

Three Layer Squares

A winning layered cookie for those who enjoy chocolate.

Cookie Crust:

¼ lb. (1 stick) butter or margarine, softened
1 egg
1 tablespoon sugar
1¼ cups flour
1 teaspoon baking powder
1 package (12 oz.) semi-sweet chocolate bits

Topping:

2 eggs
¾ cup sugar
2 teaspoons vanilla extract
6 tablespoons butter or margarine, melted and cooled
2 cups chopped pecans

In a bowl, stir together ingredients for cookie crust: butter, egg, sugar, flour and baking powder. Press mixture into bottom of 9" x 9" baking dish. Bake in preheated 350° F. oven for 10 minutes. Meanwhile, in another bowl, stir together topping ingredients: eggs, sugar, vanilla, butter and pecans; set aside.

Remove baked crust from oven and sprinkle with chocolate bits. Return to oven for 5 minutes. Again remove from oven and spread chocolate smoothly over crust. Pour topping mixture over chocolate and continue baking for another 35 minutes. Cool and cut into squares.

Makes about 2 dozen squares.

Parmesan Oven Fried Chicken

Parmesan cheese makes this crust extra crispy.

½ cup cornflake crumbs
⅓ cup grated Parmesan cheese
¼ teaspoon salt
⅛ teaspoon ground pepper
4 tablespoons butter or margarine, melted and divided
1 (2½ to 3 lbs.) broiler-fryer chicken, cut into parts

In a shallow bowl, stir together cornflake crumbs, cheese, salt and pepper. Pour 1 tablespoon butter into the bottom of a 9″ x 13″ baking pan and spread evenly to coat bottom of pan. Pour remaining butter into a shallow bowl. Dip chicken first into butter, coating on all sides, and then into crumb mixture, coating well. Place chicken parts in buttered baking pan. Bake at 400° F. for 40 to 50 minutes.

Makes 4 servings.

French Potato Salad

When potato salad is made without mayonnaise, as it is in this recipe, it keeps better for taking to picnics.

4 cups coarsely diced potatoes
2 tablespoons cider vinegar
¼ cup chopped green onion
½ medium carrot, peeled and shredded
2 tablespoons vegetable oil
¾ teaspoon celery salt
¹/₈ teaspoon ground pepper

Cook potatoes in rapidly boiling salted water until tender. Drain thoroughly and place in bowl. Sprinkle with vinegar and gently toss. Allow potatoes to cool to room temperature. Add green onion, carrot, vegetable oil, celery salt and pepper. Again, toss gently to mix well. Chill.

Makes 4 servings.

MENU

Parmesan Oven Fried Chicken

French Potato Salad

Fresh Vegetables with Mustard Sour Cream Dip

Heavenly Chocolate Brownies

Fresh Vegetables with Mustard Sour Cream Dip

Fresh vegetables with a savory dip are enjoyable both with a meal or as an appetizer.

1 cup sour cream
1 tablespoon prepared mustard
1 teaspoon lemon juice
¼ cup minced scallion
½ teaspoon Worcestershire sauce
¼ teaspoon salt
4 cups assorted cut up fresh vegetables (as carrot sticks, cauliflower buds, fresh green beans, radishes)

In a bowl, stir together sour cream, mustard, lemon juice, scallion, Worcestershire sauce and salt. Allow to stand, refrigerated, for ½ hour before serving. Serve fresh vegetables with dip.

Makes 4 servings.

Heavenly Chocolate Brownies

These brownies are for the lover of rich chocolate.

6 squares unsweetened chocolate, divided
1 cup butter or margarine
4 eggs, well beaten
2 cups sugar
1 cup flour
2 teaspoons vanilla extract
1 can (14 oz.) sweetened condensed milk
2 cups coarsely chopped walnuts

In a double boiler, melt together butter and 4 squares chocolate; cool. In a bowl, beat together eggs and cooled chocolate mixture. Slowly beat in sugar. Stir in flour and vanilla. Pour brownie mixture into greased 9″ x 13″ baking pan. Bake at 350° F. for 25 to 30 minutes. Remove from oven and cool.

For frosting, melt remaining 2 squares chocolate in top of double boiler. Remove from heat, cool slightly and stir in sweetened condensed milk. Pour mixture over cooled brownies. Sprinkle with nuts. Allow to sit for 2 hours before serving.

Makes about 2 dozen brownies.

Rotisserie Leg of Lamb

If a rotisserie is not available, lamb may be roasted in the oven on a rack in an open roasting pan.

1 rolled leg of lamb (5½ to 6 lbs.)
2 garlic cloves, peeled and very thinly sliced
½ cup red wine
¼ cup vegetable oil
1 teaspoon salt
1 teaspoon dried rosemary leaves
½ teaspoon dried Summer Savory
½ teaspoon dried thyme
⅛ teaspoon ground pepper

Make random small cuts in lamb and insert thin slices of garlic. In a small bowl, stir together wine, oil, salt, rosemary, Summer Savory, thyme and pepper. Pour liquid into a large plastic bag. Place lamb in the bag and seal well. Rotate the bag so that lamb is well coated with wine mixture. Refrigerate for at least 24 hours, turning periodically.

Place lamb on rotisserie skewer as manufacturer directs. Roast over hot coals outdoors or on indoor rotisserie. Roasting time may vary from 1½ to 2¾ hours, so use a meat thermometer to determine desired degree of doneness. Internal temperatures for lamb are: 140°F. for rare, 160°F. for medium, and 180°F. for well-done.

Makes 12 to 16 servings.

Rosemary Potatoes

The simple addition of rosemary turns boiled new potatoes into an interesting side dish.

8 or 10 new potatoes
4 tablespoons butter or margarine
1 teaspoon dried rosemary leaves
¼ teaspoon salt
dash ground pepper

Peel new potatoes and cook in rapidly boiling salted water until tender. Meanwhile, in a small saucepan, melt butter. Stir in rosemary, salt and pepper. Set aside.

Drain cooked potatoes. Pour rosemary butter over potatoes and toss gently. Return to heat until butter mixture is simmering.

Makes 4 servings.

Stuffed Zucchini

The best of freshness is in this light-flavored vegetable-stuffed zucchini.

2 medium zucchini
1 tomato, chopped
2 tablespoons butter or margarine
1 medium onion, chopped
2 tablespoons chopped green pepper
½ teaspoon dried basil leaves
½ teaspoon salt
⅛ teaspoon ground pepper
5 tablespoons fine, dry bread crumbs, divided
1 tablespoon grated Parmesan cheese

Cut zucchini in half lengthwise; remove center portion, leaving a thick shell. Chop the zucchini that was removed and place in a bowl. Stir in tomato.

In a saucepan, melt butter. Add onion and green pepper and cook until onion is tender. Stir onion mixture into zucchini-tomato mixture. Add basil, salt, pepper, 3 tablespoons crumbs and cheese. Stir well. Spoon filling into zucchini shells. Sprinkle with remaining crumbs. Place zucchini in shallow baking dish, cover, and bake at 325° F. for 30 minutes, removing cover for the last 10 minutes of baking.

Makes 4 servings.

Frozen Angel Cake with Raspberries

This is a luscious, cool and not-too-sweet dessert.

1 10-inch baked angel cake
1 quart raspberry sherbet, softened
2 packages (10 oz. each) frozen raspberries, thawed

Cut angel cake horizontally into thirds. Place bottom layer of cake on a serving plate. Top with one half of the raspberry sherbet and spread evenly. Repeat layers, ending with top layer of cake. Place cake in freezer to harden sherbet.

Meanwhile, drain raspberries. Purée fruit and strain out seeds. Slice frozen angel cake and serve with raspberry puree.

Makes 1 (10-inch) cake.

MENU

Rotisserie Leg of Lamb
Rosemary Potatoes
Stuffed Zucchini
Frozen Angel Cake with Raspberries

Chilled Poached Sole with Louis Dressing

Poached sole makes an elegant entree with delicate flavor.

2 lbs. fillet of sole
¾ cup dry white wine or dry vermouth
¾ cup water
6 thin lemon slices
3 bay leaves
¼ teaspoon whole peppercorns

Dressing

1 cup mayonnaise
¼ cup chili sauce
2 tablespoons milk
1 teaspoon Worcestershire sauce
1 tablespoon lemon juice
1 teaspoon prepared horseradish
lettuce leaves, crisped

Roll up fish fillets and place in a large, shallow fry pan. Pour wine and water into pan. Place lemon, bay leaves and peppercorns in pan. Over moderate heat, bring liquid to simmer. Cover and cook fish over low heat until tender or about 8 to 10 minutes. Remove fish from poaching liquid and chill.

To make dressing, stir together mayonnaise, chili sauce, milk, Worcestershire sauce, lemon juice and prepared horseradish in a bowl. Serve fish fillets on lettuce and top with Louis dressing.

Makes 6 servings.

Summer Rice Salad

Chilled rice should be flaked gently with a fork to separate grains just before serving.

2 tablespoons vegetable oil
1 cup chopped green onion
¾ cup long grain rice
1½ cups chicken broth
½ teaspoon fennel seed
¼ cup finely chopped celery
lettuce leaves

In a saucepan, heat oil over moderate heat. Stir in onion and cook until onion is tender. Stir in rice and then add broth and fennel seed. Cover, reduce heat to low and cook until rice is tender. Remove from heat and chill. Stir in celery. Line serving bowl with lettuce; spoon in rice salad and serve.

Makes 4 servings.

Tarragon Marinated Carrots

If whole fresh baby carrots are available, try them in place of larger carrots for their sweeter flavor.

1 lb. fresh carrots, peeled
2 tablespoons cider vinegar
5 tablespoons vegetable oil
1 teaspoon dried leaf tarragon
¼ teaspoon salt
¼ teaspoon sugar
dash ground pepper

Slice carrots thinly on the bias and cook in rapidly boiling salted water until tender. Meanwhile in a bowl, stir together vinegar, oil, tarragon, salt, sugar and pepper. Drain carrots thoroughly and stir into marinade mixture. Allow carrots to cool, stir and refrigerate, covered. Marinate carrots at least 2 hours before serving, stirring occasionally.

Makes 4 servings.

Lemon Ice Cream Pie

Refreshingly simple and delicious all year 'round.

1½ cups graham cracker crumbs
5 tablespoons sugar
⅓ cup butter or margarine, softened
½ gallon vanilla ice cream, softened
1 can (12 oz.) frozen lemonade concentrate, thawed
1 teaspoon grated lemon peel
3 tablespoons lemon juice
6 drops yellow food coloring
1 cup heavy cream, whipped
8 lemon slices

In a bowl, stir together crumbs and sugar. Blend in butter and press mixture firmly against bottom and sides of 10-inch pie pan. Bake at 375° F. for 8 minutes; cool.

In the large bowl of a mixer, beat together ice cream, lemonade concentrate, lemon peel, and lemon juice. When well blended, pour into cooled pie shell. Freeze.

At serving time, garnish pie with whipped cream and lemon slices.

Makes 8 servings.

Cutlets with Lemon and Mushrooms

This recipe may be prepared with either veal or turkey cutlets.

⅓ cup flour
1½ teaspoons salt, divided
¼ teaspoon ground pepper, divided
4 tablespoons butter or margarine
½ lb. fresh mushrooms, cleaned and sliced
4 teaspoons lemon juice
1¼ lbs. veal or turkey cutlets
¼ cup dry white wine or dry vermouth
1 tablespoon chopped parsley

In a bowl, stir together flour, 1 teaspoon salt and ⅛ teaspoon pepper. Set aside.

Over moderate heat, melt butter in fry pan. Stir in mushrooms, lemon juice and remaining salt and pepper. Cook until mushrooms are tender. Remove mushrooms from fry pan and set aside. Dip cutlets into flour mixture and then brown in fry pan in butter. Stir in white wine and then spoon in mushrooms. Bring to simmer and cook for 3 to 5 minutes, stirring continuously. Sprinkle with parsley.

Makes 4 servings.

Parslied Shells

This is a simple side dish for a light entrée.

8 ounces medium-size shell macaroni
2 tablespoons butter or margarine
1 tablespoon chopped parsley
¼ cup grated Parmesan cheese

Cook shells according to package directions; drain well. Spoon into serving dish. Pour butter over shells and sprinkle with parsley and cheese. Toss.

Makes 4 servings.

Escalloped Tomatoes

A marvelous way to enjoy the bounty of summer tomatoes.

4 tablespoons butter or margarine
1 small onion, chopped
½ cup fine, dry bread crumbs
¾ teaspoon dried basil leaves
¼ teaspoon salt
⅛ teaspoon ground pepper
4 medium tomatoes, sliced

In a saucepan, melt butter over moderate heat. Add onion and cook until translucent. Remove from heat and stir in bread crumbs, basil, salt and pepper.

In a buttered 1½-quart casserole, arrange a layer of tomato slices; sprinkle with ⅓ of the bread crumb mixture. Repeat layers twice, ending with bread crumbs. Bake at 350° F. for 30 minutes.

Makes 4 servings.

Favorite Tossed Salad

Here is a very colorful combination of salad ingredients.

1 head romaine, washed and crisped
1 can (8¾ oz.) chick peas, drained
¼ cup sliced radishes
2 medium tomatoes, cut in wedges
1 cucumber, halved and sliced

Tear lettuce into bite-size pieces and place in bowl. Top with chick peas, radishes, tomato and cucumber. Gently toss and chill thoroughly.

Makes 4 to 6 servings.

Curry Vinaigrette Dressing

Here's a light curry variation for vinaigrette dressing.

4 tablespoons vegetable oil
2 tablespoons lemon juice
1 tablespoon wine vinegar
1 garlic clove, minced
½ teaspoon salt
¼ teaspoon curry powder
⅛ teaspoon ground pepper

In a bowl, stir together all ingredients. Allow flavors to blend for at least 1 hour before serving.

Makes about ½ cup dressing.

Crème de Menthe Parfaits

This is a delightfully cool, refreshing ice cream dessert.

1 pint lemon sherbet
1 pint lime sherbet
½ cup crème de menthe
1½ tablespoons grated lime peel

In parfait, sherbet or iced tea glasses, alternate layers of sherbets with crème de menthe. Sprinkle tops with grated lime peel.

Makes 4 servings.

Kabobs on the Grill

These kabobs are equally good made with either beef or lamb.

1½ lb. boneless beef or lamb, cut into 1½ inch chunks
1 teaspoon salt
1 garlic clove, minced
4 tablespoons vegetable oil
1 tablespoon Worcestershire sauce
4 tablespoons red wine vinegar

Place meat cubes in a glass bowl. In another bowl, stir together salt, garlic, oil, Worcestershire sauce, and vinegar. Pour this mixture over meat and stir well. Refrigerate overnight or for at least 6 hours, stirring occasionally.

Remove meat from liquid and skewer on 10 to 12-inch metal skewers. Place on grill over hot coals and cook for 15 to 20 minutes, turning kabobs once during cooking.

Makes 4 servings.

Rice with Pine Nuts

If pine nuts are unavailable, substitute almonds or walnuts.

1½ cups beef broth
1 tablespoon butter or margarine
1 tablespoon lemon juice
¾ cup long grain rice
¼ cup pine nuts
2 teaspoons chopped parsley

In a heavy saucepan, bring broth to a boil. Add butter, lemon juice, rice, pine nuts and parsley. Cover and lower heat to simmer. Cook for 15 minutes or until tender.

Makes 4 servings.

Stir-Fry Carrots, Green Beans and Mushrooms

Leave it to the Orient for crispy, flavorful vegetables.

5 medium carrots, peeled and cut into thin bias slices
½ lb. fresh green beans, cut into bias pieces
2 tablespoons vegetable oil
1½ cups fresh mushroom slices
1 teaspoon soy sauce
1 teaspoon dry sherry or white wine
¼ cup chicken broth

In a saucepan of rapidly boiling water, blanch carrots and green beans; drain well. Pour oil into fry pan and place over moderately high heat. Add carrots and green beans, stirring continuously, cook for 2 minutes. Add mushrooms and continue to cook for 1 minute. Stir in soy, sherry and chicken broth. Heat until liquid comes to simmer.

Makes 4 servings.

MENU

Kabobs on the Grill

Rice with Pine Nuts

Stir-Fry Carrots, Green Beans and Mushrooms

Nectarine Charlotte

Nectarine Charlotte

This cooling dessert is a perfect finale for a summer meal.

18 to 20 ladyfingers
4 eggs, separated
½ cup sugar, divided
2 envelopes unflavored gelatin
⅓ cup cold water
1 cup nectarine purée*
2 cups heavy cream, whipped and divided
1 teaspoon vanilla

Split ladyfingers in half lengthwise. Line an 8-cup glass bowl or springform pan with ladyfingers; cover and set aside.

In a bowl, beat 2 egg yolks with 2 tablespoons sugar until thick and lemon colored; set aside. Soften gelatin in cold water; place over hot water and stir until dissolved. Add gelatin to egg yolks and stir.

In another bowl, beat egg whites with rotary beater until soft peaks form. Gradually add 6 tablespoons sugar, beating until stiff peaks form and sugar is dissolved. Gently fold egg yolk mixture, nectarine purée, ¾ of the whipped cream and vanilla into egg whites. Pour into ladyfinger-lined bowl and chill until set. Garnish with remaining whipped cream.

Makes 8 to 10 servings.

---

*NOTE: Make nectarine purée by blending ripe nectarines in the container of a blender or food processor.

Chilled Avocado Soup

Plan on small servings as this soup is wonderfully rich.

1 medium ripe avocado, peeled and cut into large pieces
½ cup cream
2 teaspoons lemon juice
¼ teaspoon salt
⅛ teaspoon ground pepper
1½ cups chicken broth

In container of blender or food processor, purée avocado with lemon juice, salt and pepper. Spoon mixture into bowl and beat in chicken broth. Chill well.

Makes 4 servings.

Cheese and Fruit Platter

This is the making of a simple summer meal. Serve with bread or crackers.

½ lb. piece semi-soft cheese as Muenster or Havarti
½ lb. piece Swiss cheese or Jarlsberg cheese
½ lb. piece Brie or other soft-ripened cheese
1 pint fresh strawberries, hulled
1 cantaloupe, peeled, seeded and cut into wedges
2 peaches, sliced
½ lb. grapes

Cut semi-soft cheese into cubes. Cut Swiss cheese into thick strips. Arrange cheeses and fruits on serving platter. Cover and leave unrefrigerated until cheeses have reached room temperature. Serve with Orange Sour Cream Dressing for fruit.

Makes 6 servings.

Orange Sour Cream Dressing

Serve this dressing with any fruit or gelatin and fruit salad.

½ cup sour cream
2½ tablespoons orange juice
2 teaspoons sugar
¼ teaspoon grated orange rind

In a bowl, stir together sour cream, orange juice, sugar and orange rind. Chill.

Makes 4 to 6 servings.

Blueberry Buckle

To make this recipe when blueberries are not in season, substitute frozen or canned blueberries.

1 cup sugar, divided
½ cup butter or margarine, divided
1 egg
¾ cup milk
2½ cups flour, divided
½ teaspoon salt
2 teaspoons baking powder
2 cups fresh blueberries, washed and well drained
½ teaspoon ground cinnamon

In a bowl, cream together ½ cup sugar and ¼ cup butter. Stir in egg and milk. In another bowl, stir together 2 cups flour, salt and baking powder. Add flour mixture to butter mixture and stir. Carefully stir in blueberries. Pour batter into 9″ x 9″ greased and floured baking pan. Spread evenly in pan.

In a small bowl, stir together remaining ½ cup sugar, remaining ½ cup flour, remaining ¼ cup butter and cinnamon. Sprinkle this mixture over top of batter. Bake at 375° F. for 40 to 50 minutes.

Makes 9 to 12 servings.

Coffee Can Batter Bread

A delicious homemade bread baked in a coffee can.

1 package dry yeast
½ cup lukewarm water
3 tablespoons sugar
1 can (15 oz.) evaporated milk
1 teaspoon salt
2 tablespoons vegetable oil
4 to 4½ cups flour
butter or margarine

In the bowl of a mixer, stir together yeast, water and 1 tablespoon sugar by hand. Let stand until bubbly or about 15 minutes. Add remaining sugar, milk, salt and oil. Beat in flour, 1 cup at a time, stirring in last cup by hand. Dough will be too sticky to knead.

Spoon bread into a well-greased 2 lb. coffee can. Cover with can lid. Let rise for 1 to 1½ hours or until lid pops off can. Bake in a preheated oven at 350° F. for 60 minutes. Brush top of bread with butter and allow to cool for 5 to 10 minutes. Loosen bread from can and cool.

Makes 1 loaf.

MENU

Chilled Avocado Soup

Cheese and Fruit Platter

Orange Sour Cream Dressing

Blueberry Buckle

Coffee Can Batter Bread

Marble-Top Chocolate Pie

Marble-Top Chocolate Pie

This is an impressive company dessert which can be prepared up to a day ahead.

¾ cup sugar, divided
1 envelope unflavored gelatin
dash salt
1⅓ cups milk
2 eggs, separated
1 package (6 oz.) semi-sweet chocolate bits
1 cup heavy cream
1 teaspoon vanilla
1 baked 9-inch pie shell

In a saucepan, stir together ½ cup sugar, gelatin and salt. Stir in milk and egg yolks. Place over moderate heat and cook, stirring continuously until slightly thickened. Stir in chocolate bits until melted. Chill until partially set.

In a bowl, beat egg whites until soft peaks form. Slowly add ¼ cup sugar and beat until whites are stiff and sugar is dissolved. Fold egg whites into chocolate mixture. In another bowl, whip together cream and vanilla until stiff.

Alternately spoon one half of the chocolate mixture and then one half of the whipped cream into the pie shell. Repeat layers. Swirl top with knife to marble. Chill until firm.

Makes 1 (9-inch) pie.

Autumn

Cream of Squash Soup

If you need to save time, use canned or frozen winter squash.

6 tablespoons butter or margarine
6 tablespoons flour
1½ cups chicken broth
½ cup light cream
2 cups milk
2 cups cooked winter squash, mashed
½ teaspoon salt
⅛ teaspoon ground pepper
1 teaspoon ground nutmeg

In a saucepan, melt butter over moderate heat. Stir in flour and cook for 5 minutes without browning flour. Beat in broth and cook until thickened. Remove from heat and stir in cream, milk, squash, salt, pepper and nutmeg. Return to heat and bring to simmer. Cool for 3 to 5 minutes, stirring continuously.

Makes 6 servings.

MENU

Cream of Squash Soup

Steak au Poivre

Baked Stuffed Potatoes

Green Beans with Ginger

Apple Upside Down Cake

Steak au Poivre

Select individual steaks at the market or purchase a piece of boneless sirloin strip or tenderloin and cut your own steaks to the desired thickness.

4 boneless individual steaks, cut ¾ to 1-inch thick
1 tablespoon whole black peppercorns, coarsely cracked
1 tablespoon butter or margarine
1 tablespoon vegetable oil
2 tablespoons minced shallots or green onion
⅓ cup cognac or brandy
¼ cup beef bouillon
1 teaspoon cornstarch

Trim fat, as necessary from steaks. Press crushed peppercorns into both sides of each steak and let steaks stand for about an hour.

In a fry pan over moderately high heat, warm butter and oil. Sauté steaks on each side until they reach desired degree of doneness. Remove from pan and keep warm.

Pour off excess fat and add shallots, cooking until they are soft. Add cognac and carefully set aflame, shaking pan until flame dies. In a small bowl, stir together bouillon and cornstarch; pour into fry pan and stir well to free any browned bits. Remove pan from heat. Pour sauce over steaks and serve.

Makes 4 servings.

Baked Stuffed Potatoes

Here's a recipe that can be prepared long ahead and frozen ready for good eating anytime. In fact, you may want to double the recipe so that you can serve half and freeze half.

4 medium baking potatoes
½ cup milk
1½ tablespoons butter or margarine
1 teaspoon salt
¼ teaspoon ground pepper
⅓ cup chopped scallion
3 tablespoons grated Parmesan cheese

Scrub and bake potatoes at 450° F. for 40 minutes. Split potatoes lengthwise and carefully scoop out inside into a large bowl, leaving potato skin shell. Set shells aside. Mash potato with milk, butter, salt and pepper until smooth. Then stir in ¼ cup scallion and cheese. Refill shells with mashed potato mixture. Bake, uncovered, for about 30 minutes at 350° F. Remove from oven, sprinkle with remaining scallion and serve.

Makes 4 servings.

Green Beans with Ginger

If there is no fresh ginger in the cupboard, substitute ¼ teaspoon ground ginger. The flavor will be different from fresh, but still very good.

1 lb. fresh green beans, cleaned and cut
3 tablespoons butter or margarine
½ teaspoon fresh, grated ginger
¼ teaspoon salt

In a saucepan, cook beans in rapidly boiling salted water until tender; drain. Meanwhile, in a fry pan, melt butter; add onion and sauté until onion is transparent. Add ginger, salt and cooked beans. Continue cooking for about 3 minutes.

Makes 4 servings.

Apple Upside Down Cake

You may never go back to pineapple upside down cake after you try this recipe.

1¼ cups butter or margarine, softened and divided
1 cup firmly-packed brown sugar
1 teaspoon ground cinnamon
7 or 8 medium apples, peeled, cored and cut into eighths
2¼ cups cake flour
1½ cups sugar
¾ cup milk
3 eggs
2½ teaspoons baking powder
1 teaspoon salt
1 teaspoon vanilla extract

Melt ½ cup butter in 9″ x 13″ baking pan on top of range. In a bowl, stir together brown sugar and cinnamon. Sprinkle evenly over butter in bottom of pan. Arrange apple slices neatly in rows over brown sugar mixture; set aside.

Place flour, sugar, milk, eggs, remaining ¾ cup butter, baking powder, salt and vanilla in the large bowl of a mixer. At low speed, beat until ingredients are well mixed, scraping bowl with rubber spatula. Beat at medium speed for 5 minutes, scraping bowl occasionally. Pour batter over apples and carefully spread mixture evenly in pan. Bake at 375° F. for 35 to 40 minutes. Remove from oven and cool for 10 minutes. Invert cake on serving plate and allow to cool completely.

Makes 1 (9″ x 13″) cake.

All-American Chicken Pot Pie

Save the extra chicken broth to make your favorite home-made soup another day.

2 tablespoons vegetable oil
1 roasting chicken (4 to 5 lb.), cut up
1 large onion, coarsely chopped
5 medium carrots, peeled
3 ribs celery, cut in large chunks
salt
ground pepper
2 bay leaves
5 tablespoons butter or margarine
⅓ cup flour
1 cup light cream
½ lb. small white onions, peeled
1 package (10 oz.) frozen peas, thawed and drained
piecrust for 1-crust pie
1 egg yolk
1 teaspoon milk

In a large sauce pot, heat oil over moderately high heat. Add chicken and brown well. Meanwhile, cut 3 carrots into large chunks. Remove browned chicken from pot and stir in onion, cut up carrots and celery. Cook until onion is tender. Return chicken to pot and add water to cover, 4 teaspoons salt, ½ teaspoon ground pepper and bay leaves. Reduce heat and simmer chicken for 1½ hours. Remove chicken from pot; set both chicken and broth aside to cool. Remove and discard chicken bones and skin. Cut meat into bite-size pieces.

In a saucepan, melt butter over moderate heat. Stir in flour and continue cooking for 3 minutes, stirring continuously, without browning flour. Gradually stir in 1½ cups cooking liquid from chicken, light cream, 1 teaspoon salt and ¼ teaspoon ground pepper. Cook, stirring, until mixture comes to a boil and thickens; remove from heat. Stir in whole onions, remaining carrots which have been cut into 1-inch thick pieces, peas and chicken. Pour mixture into 3-quart baking dish.

Roll pie crust into a piece 2 inches larger than top of baking dish. Cut vents in crust with the point of a knife. Fit crust loosely over the top of the baking dish.

In a small bowl, beat together egg yolk and milk. Gently brush top of the crust with yolk mixture. Bake pot pie at 400° F. for 45 minutes or until bubbly and crust is golden brown. **Makes 8 servings.**

MENU

All-American Chicken Pot Pie

Cranberry Apple Sauce

Red and Green Pepper Salad

Baked Oranges Grand Marnier

Cranberry Apple Sauce

This variation of traditional cranberry sauce has a lighter color and flavor.

2 cups sugar
1½ cups water
1 package (16 oz.) fresh cranberries
4 medium apples, peeled, cored and thinly sliced

In a saucepan over moderate heat, heat sugar and water to boil. Stir in cranberries and apples. Lower heat to simmer and cook, covered, for about 10 to 12 minutes or until cranberries pop and apples become very soft. Remove from heat and stir a few times. Cool.

Makes about 6 cups.

Red and Green Pepper Salad

Choose this recipe when you want a salad with color and extra-crisp texture.

2 medium green bell peppers, halved and seeded
2 medium red bell peppers, halved and seeded
2 tablespoons wine vinegar
6 tablespoons olive oil
1 teaspoon finely chopped shallots
½ teaspoon Summer Savory or rosemary
½ teaspoon salt
⅛ teaspoon ground pepper
1 head Boston lettuce, washed and crisped

Cut peppers into very thin strips; set aside. In a bowl, beat together vinegar, oil, shallots, Summer Savory, salt and pepper. Add pepper strips and toss until peppers are well coated with dressing. Line individual plates with lettuce leaves. Spoon peppers onto lettuce leaves. Pour dressing over peppers; chill.

Makes 4 servings.

Baked Oranges Grand Marnier

The perfect, luscious dessert when you need something light in flavor.

4 large oranges
2 tablespoons butter or margarine
3 tablespoons sugar
2 tablespoons Grand Marnier or Cointreau
⅓ cup orange juice

Carefully peel oranges, reserving peel, and place oranges in a baking dish. Pour butter over oranges and sprinkle with 2 tablespoons sugar. Bake at 350° F. for 10 minutes.

Meanwhile, cut some of the rind to make 1 tablespoon julienne strips. Place rind in a small saucepan with 1 tablespoon sugar, Grand Marnier and orange juice. Bring to simmer and pour over baked oranges.

Makes 4 servings.

Hot Mulled Cider

A welcome beverage on a cool day.

2 2-inch cinnamon sticks
1 teaspoon whole allspice
1 teaspoon whole cloves
2 quarts apple cider
½ cup brown sugar
dash ground nutmeg
8 extra long cinnamon sticks

Tie cinnamon, allspice, and cloves in a small piece of cheesecloth. Pour cider into a large pot. Stir in brown sugar and add spice bag. Slowly bring to simmer and cook for 10 minutes. Remove spice bag. Serve hot with a dash of nutmeg and cinnamon stick stirrer.

Makes 8 servings.

Beef 'n Beer Stew

Enjoy using the electric knife to slice onions and cut stew meat for this hearty entree.

6 strips bacon
5 cups thinly sliced onions
2 garlic cloves, minced
2 tablespoons vegetable oil
3 lbs. boneless beef, cut into 2-inch chunks or strips
2 tablespoons flour
2 cups beer
1 cup beef bouillon
1½ teaspoons sugar
1 teaspoon dried thyme
2 bay leaves
2 tablespoons red wine vinegar
¾ teaspoon salt
¼ teaspoon ground pepper

In a large saucepan or Dutch oven, cook bacon over moderate heat until crisp. Remove bacon and drain. Pour off all but ¼ cup bacon drippings. Add onions and garlic to the pan, cooking until onions are tender, stirring frequently. Remove onions from pan. Pour oil into the pan and stir in meat, cooking until meat is well browned on all sides. Stir in flour and cook for 2 minutes. Return onions to the pan. Pour in beer and bouillon; add sugar, thyme, bay leaves, vinegar, salt and pepper.

Cover and simmer slowly for 1½ to 2 hours or until meat is tender. Skim off any excess fat before serving. Crumble bacon and serve as garnish on stew.

Makes 6 servings.

MENU

Hot Mulled Cider
Beef 'n Beer Stew
Herbed Potatoes
French Fried Zucchini
Buttered Beets with Mustard
Walnut Pie

Herbed Potatoes

Here is a potato dish you can prepare in just 10 minutes.

4 tablespoons butter or margarine
¼ teaspoon dried thyme leaves
2 teaspoons chopped parsley
3 cups coarsely diced, peeled cooked potatoes
¼ teaspoon salt
dash ground pepper
¼ teaspoon paprika

Melt butter in a saucepan. Stir in thyme and parsley. Add potatoes, salt, pepper and paprika. Cook for about 10 minutes or until potatoes are thoroughly heated, tossing potatoes gently in herbed butter.

Makes 6 servings.

French Fried Zucchini

This needn't be saved for last-minute cooking. Once fried, zucchini can be kept in a warm oven for about 20 to 30 minutes.

2 medium zucchini
1 egg, slightly beaten
⅔ cup fine, dry bread crumbs
1 teaspoon dried leaf basil
1 teaspoon dried leaf oregano
oil for frying
1 teaspoon salt

Wash and cut zucchini into sticks. In a small bowl, beat egg with 1 tablespoon water. In another bowl, mix together bread crumbs, basil, and oregano. Dust zucchini sticks in flour. Then dip in egg mixture and finally in crumb mixture. Set aside for 15 to 20 minutes. Deep fry in hot oil until golden brown; drain. Sprinkle with salt and serve.

Makes 4 servings.

Buttered Beets with Mustard

This is a full-flavored vegetable combination for any season.

1 bunch fresh beets (about 1½ to 2 lbs.)
5 tablespoons butter or margarine
1 tablespoon prepared mustard
½ teaspoon dried leaf tarragon

In a saucepan in rapidly boiling salted water, cook beets in their jackets until tender. Drain, peel and slice beets. Return beets to the saucepan with butter, prepared mustard and tarragon. Simmer over low heat until all ingredients are thoroughly combined and warm.

Makes 4 to 6 servings.

Walnut Pie

Enjoy pecan pie? Try this delicious dessert.

3 eggs
1 cup dark corn syrup
⅔ cup sugar
¼ cup butter or margarine, melted
2 teaspoons vanilla extract
1 cup coarsely chopped walnuts
1 9-inch unbaked pie shell

In a bowl, beat eggs well with mixer. Beat in corn syrup, sugar, butter and vanilla. Stir in walnuts and pour mixture into a pie shell. Bake at 350° F. for 1 hour or until knife inserted 1 inch from the edge comes out clean. Cool.

Makes 8 servings.

Ham Stuffed Mushrooms

These stuffed mushrooms are excellent as hors d'oeuvres or as a first course.

16 large fresh mushrooms, cleaned
4 tablespoons butter or margarine
¼ cup chopped onion
2 ounces ham, chopped
3 tablespoons grated Parmesan cheese
2 tablespoons fine, dry bread crumbs
½ cup sour cream

Remove stems from mushrooms; set caps aside. Chop stems. Over moderate heat, melt butter in a saucepan. Stir in chopped mushrooms and onion. Cook, stirring frequently for 5 minutes. Remove from heat and stir in ham, cheese and crumbs. Spoon ham mixture into mushroom caps, placing caps on a baking sheet. Place a small spoonful of sour cream on top of each stuffed mushroom. Bake at 375° F. for 15 to 20 minutes.

Makes 4 appetizer servings.

Fish Steaks with Fresh Tomato Sauce

The abundance and flavor of tomatoes in early fall makes this a special recipe of the season.

2 tablespoons butter or margarine
1 small onion, peeled and finely chopped
3 medium tomatoes, peeled, seeded and chopped
½ teaspoon dried basil leaves
¼ teaspoon salt
dash ground pepper
2 tablespoons vegetable oil
4 fish steaks, cut 1-inch thick (halibut, swordfish, cod)

Melt butter in a saucepan. Add onions and cook over moderate heat until onions are tender. Add tomatoes, basil, salt and pepper. Cover and simmer for 10 minutes. Remove lid and simmer until most of the liquid has evaporated.

While tomato sauce is simmering, dip fish steaks in oil on both sides and place on broiling pan rack. Broil for 5 minutes on each side or until lightly browned. Top with tomato sauce and serve.

Makes 4 servings.

Home Fries

Here's a wonderful dish for using leftover potatoes.

3 tablespoons bacon drippings or butter
4 medium potatoes, cooked and sliced or coarsely chopped
1 medium onion, thinly sliced
To taste salt and pepper

In a large fry pan over moderate heat, melt bacon drippings. Add potato slices and onion. Cook for about 10 minutes or until potatoes brown; stir or turn occasionally. Sprinkle with salt and pepper.

Makes 4 servings.

Piquant Brussel Sprouts

This recipe combines a full-flavored vegetable and a zesty topping.

1 lb. brussel sprouts, trimmed and cut in half
1½ tablespoons butter or margarine, melted
1 teaspoon prepared mustard
¼ teaspoon Worcestershire sauce
¼ teaspoon salt
¼ teaspoon dried basil leaves

Cook brussel sprouts in a saucepan in rapidly boiling salted water until tender; drain. Pour melted butter over sprouts. Stir in mustard, Worcestershire sauce, salt and basil. Return pan to moderate heat and cook for 1 to 2 minutes, stirring.

Makes 4 servings.

MENU

Ham Stuffed Mushrooms

Fish Steaks with Fresh Tomato Sauce

Home Fries

Piquant Brussel Sprouts

Raisin Gingerbread with Cinnamon Whipped Cream

Raisin Gingerbread with Cinnamon Whipped Cream

This old-fashioned dessert is dressed up with a cool, cinnamon topping.

1 package gingerbread mix
½ cup seedless raisins
1 cup heavy cream
2 tablespoons powdered sugar
½ teaspoon vanilla extract
½ teaspoon ground cinnamon

Prepare gingerbread according to package directions, stirring raisins into batter. Bake as directed and cool.

In a bowl, whip cream until stiff with powdered sugar, vanilla and cinnamon. Serve squares of gingerbread topped with a spoonful of cinnamon whipped cream.

Makes 9 servings.

Stuffed Crown Roast of Pork

Be sure to give your meatman several days notice to prepare the roast and plan on 2 ribs per person.

1 (14 to 16 rib) pork crown roast

Place roast, rib ends down, on a rack in an open roasting pan. Roast at 325° F. for 2 hours. Meanwhile, prepare stuffing. Remove roast from the oven; invert so rib ends are up. Fill center of roast with stuffing. Return to the oven and continue roasting for 1½ hours or until internal temperature reaches 170° F. Remove roast from the oven and allow to rest for 15 minutes before carving.

Makes 7 to 8 servings.

Sausage and Chestnut Stuffing

This rich, hearty stuffing goes beautifully with pork or poultry.

1 lb. pork sausage meat
2 tablespoons vegetable oil
1 cup chopped onion
½ cup chopped celery
3 cups fresh bread crumbs
1 lb. fresh chestnuts, shelled and peeled, coarsely chopped
1 teaspoon salt
¼ teaspoon ground pepper

In a fry pan over moderate heat, cook sausage, breaking up pieces with a fork. Remove from pan when well browned and place in a large bowl. Add oil to fry pan and return to heat. Add onion and celery, cooking until onion is tender. Add onion-celery mixture to sausage. Stir in bread crumbs, chestnuts, salt and pepper.

Makes 6 to 8 cups stuffing.

Honey Baked Squash

If there's no honey in the cupboard, use ⅔ cup packed brown sugar instead.

2 medium acorn squash
4 tablespoons butter or margarine, melted
6 tablespoons honey
½ teaspoon ground nutmeg

Cut squash in half lengthwise and remove seeds and stringy portion. Arrange squash halves, cut–side–down on greased baking sheet. Bake at 375° F. for 45 minutes. Remove from oven, pour melted butter and honey over flesh of squash. Sprinkle with nutmeg. Return to oven for an additional 5 minutes.

Makes 4 servings.

Savory Baked Cucumbers

Here's a wonderful new way to enjoy cucumbers — as a hot vegetable.

4 medium cucumbers
1 teaspoon salt
1 tablespoon cider vinegar
2 tablespoons butter or margarine, melted
2 tablespoons minced onion
1 tablespoon chopped parsley
½ teaspoon dried basil leaves

Peel cucumbers and cut in half lengthwise; scoop out seeds. Cut cucumbers crosswise into 1-inch thick slices. In a bowl, toss cucumber with salt and vinegar and let stand for 30 minutes; drain well. Place cucumbers in a baking dish with butter, onion, parsley, and basil. Bake, covered at 375° F. for 1 hour, stirring once or twice during baking.

Makes 4 servings.

Native and Cress Salad

If you're not familiar with the taste of watercress, try it before tossing into salad. You may want to vary the amount of this full-flavored salad green.

1 head Boston lettuce, washed and crisped
1 bunch watercress, washed and crisped
1 head Belgian endive
2 tablespoons wine vinegar
6 tablespoons olive oil
1 teaspoon minced shallots
¼ teaspoon salt
dash ground pepper
1 tablespoon minced chives

Tear lettuce into bite-size pieces and place in bowl. Break watercress into bite-size pieces and add to lettuce. Cut endive into 1-inch pieces and separate leaves. Add to other greens. Toss gently and chill.

In a small bowl, stir together vinegar, oil, shallots, salt and pepper. To serve, pour dressing over salad greens, toss gently and sprinkle with chives.

Makes 4 servings.

MENU

Stuffed Crown Roast of Pork

Sausage and Chestnut Stuffing

Honey Baked Squash

Savory Baked Cucumbers

Native and Cress Salad

Hazelnut Soufflé

Hazelnut Soufflé

Because hazelnuts are only plentiful in the fall and you may want to make this special dessert year 'round, simply substitute always-available walnuts.

3 tablespoons butter or margarine, divided
9 tablespoons sugar
3 tablespoons flour
¾ cup milk
5 eggs, separated
2 tablespoons vanilla extract
½ cup pulverized toasted hazelnuts*
powdered sugar

Butter the inside of a 6-cup soufflé dish, using 1 tablespoon of butter. Spoon 3 tablespoons of sugar into dish. Rotating dish, coat the inside evenly with the sugar; set aside.

In a saucepan, beat flour with ¼ cup of the milk; then, beat in remaining milk. Add 5 tablespoons of sugar and stir mixture over moderate heat until liquid thickens and comes to a boil. Boil for ½ minute and remove from heat. Allow mixture to cool for 5 minutes. Beat in 4 egg yolks, one at a time. Then beat in remaining 2 tablespoons of butter.

In a large bowl, beat egg whites until soft peaks form. Sprinkle with remaining 1 tablespoon of sugar and continue beating until stiff peaks form. Stir ¼ of the egg whites into the egg yolk mixture. Then stir in vanilla and nuts. Gently fold remaining whites into egg yolk mixture. Pour into a soufflé dish and bake in preheated 375° F. oven for 50 to 55 minutes. Serve immediately, dusted with powdered sugar.

Makes 4 servings.

---

*Note: Hazelnuts are also called filberts.

Roast Stuffed Turkey

When deciding on the size of turkey for your dinner, plan on 1 pound of turkey per person and ¾ cup stuffing per pound.

Remove giblets of fresh or thawed turkey, rinse. Pack stuffing lightly into bird and close with skewers and string; truss. Tie wings to breast of turkey with string. Place turkey, breast side up, on a rack in a shallow open roasting pan. Brush skin with melted butter or margarine. Place in 325° F. oven and roast according to timetable below:

Oven-Ready Weight	Approximate Total Cooking Time
4 to 8	3 to 4½
8 to 12	4 to 4¾
12 to 16	4½ to 5
16 to 20	6 to 7
20 to 24	6½ to 8½

Internal temperature should be 180 to 185° F. Use meat thermometer inserted into thickest part of thigh, not touching bone.

After cooking, allow turkey to rest for about 20 minutes before carving.

Cornbread and Oyster Stuffing

Fresh oysters complement the light sweetness of cornbread stuffing.

2 packages (8½ oz., each) corn muffin mix
3 eggs
⅔ cup milk
1 cup chopped onion
1 cup chopped celery
1 cup butter or margarine
¾ cup chicken broth
½ pint oysters
1 teaspoon salt

Prepare corn muffin mix according to package directions, using 2 eggs and milk. Meanwhile, melt butter in a saucepan. Add onion and celery and cook until onions are translucent. Remove from heat. In a large bowl, crumble cooked cornbread. Stir in onion-celery mixture, remaining egg, oysters and salt.

Makes 9 cups stuffing, enough for a 9 to 12 pound turkey.

MENU

Roast Stuffed Turkey

Cornbread and Oyster Stuffing

Giblet Gravy

Caramelized Onions

Broccoli Parmesan

Pineapple Lemon Gelatin Salad

Pumpkin Rum Pie

Giblet Gravy

Depending upon the size of the turkey, giblets may take more simmering time before they are tender.

turkey giblets
1 medium onion, chopped
1 rib celery, cut up
1 medium carrot, peeled and cut up
1 teaspoon salt
¼ teaspoon ground pepper
6 tablespoons flour

In a saucepan over moderate heat, simmer neck, giblets, liver and gizzard of turkey with onion, celery, carrot, salt and pepper in enough water to cover for about 30 minutes or until tender. Remove giblets and vegetables from saucepan and reserve cooking liquid. Chop giblets. Remove meat from neck and chop. Discard bones and cooking vegetables.

Pour cooking juices from turkey roasting pan into a large bowl, scraping pan for all browned bits. Spoon 6 tablespoons fat from turkey cooking juices into a large saucepan and place over moderate heat. Stir in flour and cook, stirring continuously, for about 5 minutes without browning flour. Measure cooking juices with enough reserved cooking liquid from giblets to make 4 cups. Pour liquid into a saucepan and cook until gravy thickens. Stir in chopped giblets and neck meat. Season to taste with salt and pepper.

Makes about 4 cups gravy.

Caramelized Onions

Caramelized sugar gives onion just a light touch of sweetness.

½ **cup sugar**
5½ **tablespoons boiling water**
1 **lb. small whole onions, peeled and cooked**

In a heavy saucepan over moderately high heat, bring sugar and 2½ tablespoons water to a boil, swirling pan by handle over heat until sugar is dissolved. Continue cooking until sugar turns light brown, swirling frequently. Remove saucepan from heat and very carefully and slowly stir in remaining 3 tablespoons boiling water. Then add onions and return saucepan to heat onions thoroughly.

Makes 4 servings.

Broccoli Parmesan

Broccoli will not hold well once it is cooked, so be sure it is one of the last foods prepared for the meal.

1 **bunch fresh broccoli**
6 **tablespoons butter or margarine, melted**
¼ **cup grated Parmesan cheese**
1 **tablespoon lemon juice**

Wash and trim broccoli. Cook in a saucepan in rapidly boiling salted water until tender. Stir together butter, cheese and lemon juice. Pour over cooked broccoli.

Makes 4 to 6 servings.

MENU

Roast Stuffed Turkey

Cornbread and Oyster Stuffing

Giblet Gravy

Caramelized Onions

Broccoli Parmesan

Pineapple Lemon Gelatin Salad

Pumpkin Rum Pie

Pineapple Lemon Gelatin Salad

If you make this salad in a ring mold, plan to fill the center with pineapple chunks and additional orange slices.

1 package (3 oz.) cream cheese, softened
½ cup light cream
1 package (6 oz.) lemon-flavored gelatin
2 cups boiling water
½ cup cold water
1 can (8¼ oz.) crushed pineapple, drained
2 oranges, peeled and sliced
lettuce leaves

In a small bowl, beat together cream cheese and light cream; set aside.

Dissolve gelatin in boiling water in a large bowl. Stir in cream cheese mixture, cold water and crushed pineapple. Arrange orange slices at bottom of a 1½-quart mold. Spoon a small amount of lemon gelatin mixture over oranges; chill until set. Pour remaining lemon gelatin into mold. Chill until gelatin is firm. Unmold on lettuce and serve.

Makes 8 to 10 servings.

Pumpkin Rum Pie

Enjoy the full flavor of this pie with cool whipped cream as a garnish.

1½ cups canned or mashed cooked pumpkin
¾ cup sugar
½ teaspoon salt
1 cup milk
½ cup light cream
⅓ cup dark rum
3 eggs, slightly beaten
1¼ teaspoons ground cinnamon
½ teaspoon ground ginger
½ teaspoon ground nutmeg
¼ teaspoon ground cloves
1 unbaked 9-inch pie shell

In a large bowl, beat together pumpkin, sugar, salt, milk, light cream, rum, eggs, cinnamon, ginger, nutmeg and cloves. Pour into a pie shell and bake at 400° F. for 50 minutes or until knife inserted near side of filling comes out clean. Cool.

Makes 1 (9-inch) pie.

MENU

Roast Stuffed Turkey

Cornbread and Oyster Stuffing

Giblet Gravy

Caramelized Onions

Broccoli Parmesan

Pineapple Lemon Gelatin Salad

Pumpkin Rum Pie

Broiled Ham Steak with Mustard Honey Glaze

This recipe may be a good one to try when you have leftover baked ham that can be thickly sliced for broiling.

¼ **cup honey**
2 **teaspoons prepared Dijon-type mustard**
½ **teaspoon soy sauce**
1 **fully cooked 1-inch thick ham slice (about 1½ lbs.)**

In a small bowl, stir together honey, mustard and soy sauce.

Trim excess fat from ham. Slash edge of ham at 2-inch intervals so that it won't curl during cooking. Place ham slice on rack of broiler pan. Place under broiler and cook so that meat is lightly browned. Remove from broiler, brush with mustard-honey mixture and continue to broil until glaze browns. Turn ham and broil on other side, again brushing with glaze.

Makes 4 servings.

Orange Sweet Potato Casserole

This recipe is a favorite for making the day ahead. Simply put mashed sweets into casserole and refrigerate until ready to bake. Then add twenty minutes to the baking time.

2 **lbs. sweet potatoes or yams**
1 **teaspoon grated orange rind**
2 **tablespoons butter or margarine**
¼ **cup brown sugar, packed**
16 **marshmallows**

Peel and cube sweet potatoes and cook in boiling water until tender. Drain and mash sweet potatoes with orange rind, butter and brown sugar.Spoon potatoes into buttered 1½-quart casserole. Bake for 15 minutes at 300° F.; remove from oven and top with marshmallows. Return to oven only until marshmallows begin to melt.

Makes 4 servings.

French-Style Peas

When fresh peas aren't available, substitute two 10-ounce packages of frozen peas.

3½ lbs. fresh green peas, shelled
3 tablespoons butter or margarine
3 tablespoons minced scallion
½ teaspoon salt
1 small head Boston lettuce

Cook peas in rapidly boiling salted water in saucepan for 5 to 10 minutes or until tender; drain. Meanwhile in another saucepan, melt butter over moderate heat. Add scallion and salt and cook until scallion is tender. Stir in lettuce leaves and cooked peas. Cook briefly until all ingredients are thoroughly heated.

Makes 6 servings.

Bread and Butter Pudding

To vary the flavor, if you'd like, add nuts, lemon rind or orange rind.

2 cups milk
2 eggs, slightly beaten
½ cup brown sugar
1 teaspoon vanilla extract
½ cup raisins
2½ tablespoons butter or margarine, softened
6 slices bread

In a large bowl, beat together milk and eggs. Stir in brown sugar, vanilla and raisins. Spread butter on bread slices; tear bread into 1-inch cubes and place in a bowl with egg mixture. Stir thoroughly and pour into 1-quart baking dish. Place baking dish in a shallow pan filled with 1 inch of water. Bake at 350° F. for about 45 minutes or until knife inserted in center comes out clean.

Makes 4 to 6 servings.

MENU

Broiled Ham Steak with Mustard Honey Glaze

Orange Sweet Potato Casserole

French-Style Peas

Bread and Butter Pudding

Provençal Fish Stew

Select 2 varieties of fish for stew, using either fillets or boneless steaks. For example, you may want to try cod and swordfish for different flavors.

3 tablespoons vegetable oil
1 cup chopped onion
1 garlic clove, minced
1 cup chopped, peeled and seeded tomatoes
1½ teaspoons salt
¼ teaspoon dried leaf thyme
¼ teaspoon fennel seed
¼ teaspoon ground pepper
dash ground saffron
1½ lbs. boneless fish
8 littleneck clams
8 mussels
3 cups water

In a large saucepan, heat oil over moderate heat. Add onion and garlic, cooking until onion is tender. Stir in tomatoes, salt, thyme, fennel, pepper and saffron. Cook, covered, for 3 minutes. Add fish, clams, mussels and water. Cover pot and bring to boil. Reduce heat and simmer for 10 to 15 minutes.

Makes 4 entrée-size servings.

Garlic Croutons

These croutons are delicious as toast as well as a flavorful garnish for soup.

4 tablespoons butter or margarine
1 garlic clove, minced
1 teaspoon chopped parsley
8 slices French bread

Melt butter in a saucepan over moderate heat. Stir in garlic and parsley. Cook for 3 minutes; remove from heat. Brush bread slices on both sides with garlic butter and place on baking sheet. Broil bread until golden brown. Turn and broil on the other side.

Makes 8 croutons.

Tossed Green Salad .

Favorite for dinner.

½ small iceberg lettuce, crisped
¼ head chicory, crisped
1 cup alfalfa sprouts
2 tomatoes, cut into wedges
12 pitted ripe olives
¼ cup shredded Cheddar cheese

Into a serving bowl, tear iceberg and chicory into bite-size pieces. Top with sprouts and toss gently. Arrange tomato wedges and olives on top of lettuce. Sprinkle with cheese. Serve with your choice of dressing.

Makes 4 servings.

MENU

Provencal Fish Stew
Garlic Croutons
Tossed Green Salad
Chocolate Apricot Cake

Chocolate Apricot Cake

This cake is wonderfully moist and keeps well for several days.

5 squares unsweetened chocolate
½ cup butter or margarine
1½ cups sugar
2 eggs, slightly beaten
2 cups cake flour
2 teaspoons baking powder
½ teaspoon salt
1 cup milk
3 teaspoons vanilla extract
⅓ cup apricot preserves
2 tablespoons apricot brandy
¾ cup sour cream
1 box (1 lb.) powdered sugar

Melt 3 squares of chocolate in the top of a double boiler; cool. In the large bowl of a mixer, cream together butter and sugar until fluffy. Beat in eggs. Sift together flour, baking powder and salt. Add flour mixture alternately with milk, mixing well. Add vanilla and beat cake batter for 5 minutes at medium speed. Pour into two 9-inch greased and floured cake pans. Bake at 350° F. for 35 to 40 minutes. Cool.

In a small saucepan, stir together preserves and brandy. Heat to simmer and remove from heat.

For frosting, melt remaining chocolate in the top of a double boiler; cool. In a mixer bowl, beat sour cream, vanilla, and salt. Gradually add sugar and beat until smooth. Add cooled chocolate and continue beating for about 1 minute.

To assemble cake: cut each layer in half horizontally. Place 1 layer on serving plate. Brush with apricot glaze and top with some frosting. Repeat with remaining layers until all are glazed and frosted. With remaining frosting, ice sides of cake. Allow cake to sit for 2 hours before serving.

Makes about 10 servings.

Lentil Soup

This recipe simmers up a rich, hearty soup without the fuss of making a stock.

4 strips bacon
1 large onion, chopped
3 medium carrots, peeled and sliced
3 ribs celery, washed and sliced
1 package (16 oz.) dried lentils
8 cups water
4 teaspoons instant beef bouillon granules
2 bay leaves
¼ teaspoon whole peppercorns
1 teaspoon salt

In a large pot, cook bacon over moderate heat. Remove bacon and drain. Cook onion, carrot, and celery in bacon drippings for about 5 minutes. Stir in lentils, water, bouillon granules, bay leaves, peppercorns and salt. Bring to a boil; reduce heat and simmer for 1 hour. Chop bacon and sprinkle on each serving.

Makes 8 servings.

Curry of Lamb

The full flavor of this curry is developed by using your own spice mixture rather than prepared curry powder.

½ cup vegetable oil
1 cup finely chopped onion
2 garlic cloves, minced
1 teaspoon grated fresh ginger root
1½ lbs. boneless lamb, cut into 1-inch cubes
1 teaspoon salt
1 teaspoon ground cumin
1 teaspoon turmeric
1 teaspoon ground coriander
¼ teaspoon ground hot red pepper
¼ teaspoon ground fennel
⅛ teaspoon ground clove
⅛ teaspoon ground cinnamon
1 cup finely chopped peeled fresh tomatoes
½ cup unflavored yogurt
½ cup water

Heat ¼ cup oil in a fry pan over moderately high heat. Add onion, garlic and ginger root, cooking until onions are tender. Remove onion mixture from fry pan and set aside. Heat remaining oil in pan and add lamb. Brown meat well on all sides. Return onion mixture to pan. Stir in remaining ingredients, except yogurt and water. Cook for an additional 5 minutes, stirring occasionally. Add yogurt and water, bring to simmer and cook, covered, for 1½ to 2 hours or until meat is tender.

Makes 4 servings.

Rice with Currants

The mild flavor of this rice with sweetness from the currants makes it an excellent complement for the spiciness of Curried Lamb.

4 tablespoons butter or margarine
1 cup long grain rice
1 teaspoon salt
¼ cup currants
2 cups chicken broth

In a saucepan, melt butter over moderate heat. Add rice and cook for 3 to 5 minutes. Add salt, currants and chicken broth. Cover and simmer for about 20 minutes or until all liquid is absorbed. Stir and serve.

Makes 6 servings.

Crisp Spinach Salad

Enjoy all of the textures of this salad.

1 package (10 oz.) fresh spinach, washed and trimmed
¼ lb. fresh mushrooms, trimmed and sliced
½ cup sliced okra
12 cherry tomatoes
¼ cup seasoned croutons

In a bowl, toss together spinach, mushrooms, okra slices and tomatoes; chill. Top with croutons and a favorite dressing. Toss and serve.

Makes 4 servings.

Bananas Foster

Preparing Bananas Foster at the table can be fun for both guests and the cook. It's a showy dessert without being too difficult.

¼ cup butter or margarine
½ cup firmly packed brown sugar
4 medium bananas, peeled and halved lengthwise
⅓ cup dark rum
1 quart vanilla ice cream

In a fry pan, melt butter over moderate heat. Add brown sugar and stir until dissolved. Add bananas and sauté gently on both sides. Pour in rum and carefully set aflame. Baste bananas with rum-butter until flame dies. Serve immediately over ice cream.

Makes 4 servings.

Fish Chowder

Enjoy a New England specialty that is simple to make with either fresh or frozen fish.

3 tablespoons butter or margarine
¾ cup chopped onion
1½ lb. cod fish, cut into chunks
3 medium potatoes, peeled, diced and cooked
3 cups milk
1 cup light cream
2 bay leaves
1 teaspoon salt
¼ teaspoon ground pepper

Melt butter in a saucepan over moderate heat. Add onion and cook until onion is transparent. Stir in fish and cook for another 3 minutes. Add milk, cream, bay leaves, salt and pepper. Bring to simmer and cook over low heat for 10 minutes.

Makes 6 servings.

MENU

Fish Chowder

Yankee Pot Roast

Oven Browned Potatoes

Braised Carrots and Celery

Cauliflower with Chive Cheese Sauce

Lemon-Lime Meringue Pie

Yankee Pot Roast

To avoid last minute rush, pot roast may be cooked ahead of time, sliced and reheated in the gravy.

2 tablespoons vegetable oil
1 (3 to 4 lb.) chuck or rump pot roast
1 medium onion, peeled and thinly sliced
3 medium carrots, peeled and sliced ¼-inch thick
3 ribs celery, sliced ¼-inch thick
1½ teaspoons salt
2 bay leaves
½ teaspoon dried leaf thyme
¼ teaspoon ground pepper
¼ cup flour

Heat oil in a large sauce pot over moderate heat. Brown pot roast on all sides in oil. Remove meat from pot and set aside. Add onion, carrot and celery to pot. Cook, stirring occasionally, until onion is tender. Return meat to pot. Add 1½ cups water, salt, bay leaves, thyme and pepper; cover and reduce heat to simmer. Cook for 2½ to 3 hours or until meat is fork tender.

Remove meat and vegetables from the pot and place on a warm platter. Skim most of the fat from cooking liquid. Add water to liquid to make 1½ cups. In a small bowl, beat together flour and ⅓ cup water. Stirring continuously, add flour-water mixture to cooking liquid while simmering over moderate heat. Cook until mixture thickens. Return vegetables to gravy. Pour vegetable gravy over sliced pot roast.

Makes 8 servings.

Oven Browned Potatoes

These potatoes may be roasted in butter or in the pan drippings of a beef or pork roast.

6 medium potatoes, peeled
⅓ cup butter or margarine
dash paprika

In a saucepan, cook potatoes for 10 minutes in rapidly boiling salted water; drain. Melt butter in a shallow baking pan. Add potatoes to melted butter, turning to coat evenly. Sprinkle with paprika. Bake for 40 minutes at 325° F., turning occasionally.

Makes 6 servings.

Braised Carrots and Celery

You'll be astonished how interesting carrots and celery can taste.

3 tablespoons butter or margarine
4 medium carrots, peeled and cut in julienne pieces
5 ribs celery, cut in julienne pieces
¾ cup consommé
¼ teaspoon salt
¼ teaspoon dried leaf thyme

In a saucepan, melt butter. Add carrots and celery; sauté for 3 minutes. Add consommé, salt and thyme. Cover and cook for 10 minutes or until tender.

Makes 6 servings.

Cauliflower with Chive Cheese Sauce

The sauce is so simple to make and looks especially elegant for company when served over a whole cooked head of cauliflower.

1 head cauliflower
1 package (3 oz.) cream cheese, softened
½ cup milk
⅛ teaspoon salt
3 drops hot red pepper sauce
1½ tablespoons chopped chives, divided

Cook cauliflower whole or as flowerets in rapidly boiling salted water until tender; drain. Meanwhile, in a small saucepan, warm cream cheese, milk, salt and red pepper sauce over moderate heat. Stir continuously until mixture is smooth. Add 1 tablespoon chives and cook for 2 more minutes. Serve cream cheese sauce over hot cauliflower. Sprinkle with remaining chives.

Makes 6 servings.

Lemon-Lime Meringue Pie

A delicious break from the lemon meringue pie tradition.

1 9-inch pie crust, baked
1½ cups sugar, divided
⅓ cup cornstarch
1½ cups warm water
½ teaspoon grated lemon peel
½ teaspoon grated lime peel
¼ cup lemon juice
¼ cup lime juice
4 eggs, separated
2 tablespoons butter or margarine
¼ teaspoon salt

In a saucepan, stir together 1 cup sugar and cornstarch. Stir in water, lemon peel, lime peel, lemon juice and lime juice. Place over moderate heat and cook until mixture thickens, stirring continuously. Remove from heat.

In a small bowl, beat egg yolks. Stir a small amount of lemon-lime mixture into yolks. Then slowly pour egg mixture back into lemon-lime mixture, stirring continuously. Return to heat. Cook, stirring, to just below boil; remove from heat. Stir in butter. Pour into pie shell.

Make meringue by beating egg whites with salt until soft peaks form. Beating at high speed of mixer, add remaining sugar, 1 tablespoon at a time. Continue beating until sugar is dissolved and egg whites stand in stiff peaks. Spread meringue over pie filling, sealing the crust around edges. Bake at 400° F. for 10 minutes or until meringue browns. Cool away from draft.

Makes 1 (9-inch) pie.

Winter

Double Consommé with Julienne Vegetables

A light appetizer for a rich meal.

2 cans (10½ oz., each) condensed beef consommé
4 tablespoons dry sherry
1 cup water
1 medium carrot, peeled and cut into thin julienne strips
1 celery rib, cut into thin julienne strips

In a large saucepan, stir together consommé, sherry and water. Bring to simmer and add carrot and celery. Simmer, covered, for 10 minutes.

Makes 4 servings.

Duck with Green Peppercorn Sauce

Green peppercorns may be found in the specialty food section of the supermarket or in a specialty food store.

1 duck (4 lb.)
1¼ cups regular-strength beef broth
3 tablespoons green peppercorns, drained and rinsed
½ teaspoon dried leaf thyme
3 tablespoons flour
1 tablespoon cognac
2 tablespoons light cream

Pierce skin of duck every few inches with tines of sharp fork. Place duck on a rack in an open roasting pan. Roast at 350° F. for 1¾ to 2 hours.

Meanwhile, in a small bowl, stir together beef broth, peppercorns and thyme. Remove duck from the oven and place on a heated platter. Pour off fat and pan drippings, reserving 3 tablespoons duck fat and all of the cooking juices. Pour reserved duck fat into a saucepan and place over moderate heat. Stir in flour and cook, stirring continuously, for 5 minutes without browning flour. Stir in beef broth mixture and cooking juices from duck. Cook until mixture thickens. Add cognac and simmer for 3 minutes. Then stir in light cream and cook for another minute. Serve this sauce over carved duck.

Makes 4 servings.

Baked Herbed Rice

Here's a rice dish you can make in a few minutes, put in the oven and forget about.

1 cup long grain rice
2 tablespoons butter or margarine, melted
1 can (10½ oz.) condensed beef consommé, undiluted
⅓ cup water
½ cup sliced water chestnuts
½ cup chopped green onion
½ teaspoon dried leaf thyme

Place rice in a 1½ quart casserole. Stir in butter, consommé, water, water chestnuts, scallion and thyme. Cover and bake at 350° F. for 30 minutes. Fluff with fork.

Makes 6 servings.

Braised Belgian Endive

Endive may be split in half lengthwise or left whole for braising.

8 medium Belgian endive
2 tablespoons butter or margarine
½ cup chicken broth
2 tablespoons minced carrot

Trim base of endive and discard any outer wilted leaves. Over moderate heat, melt butter in a large fry pan. Add endive and sauté on all sides for 5 minutes. Add broth and carrot. Cover and simmer for about 10 minutes or until tender.

Makes 4 servings.

Native Lettuce with Roquefort Vinaigrette

Roquefort Vinaigrette dressing is lighter than the usual creamy blue-veined cheese dressings.

1 head Boston lettuce, washed and crisped
2 tablespoons lemon juice
6 tablespoons olive oil
½ teaspoon salt
⅛ teaspoon ground pepper
1 teaspoon minced shallots
¼ cup crumbled Roquefort or blue cheese

Tear lettuce into bite-size pieces and place in a bowl. In a small bowl, beat together lemon juice, oil, salt and pepper. Stir in shallots and cheese. Chill both lettuce and dressing thoroughly. Pour dressing over lettuce to serve.

Makes 4 servings.

Pears in Port

This dessert is very attractive when served in glass bowls or on glass plates. Garnish with a slice of lemon.

1 cup sugar
¾ cup water
½ stick cinnamon
3 whole cloves
1 cup port wine
½ teaspoon grated orange peel
½ teaspoon grated lemon peel
4 medium pears, peeled

In a saucepan over moderate heat, bring sugar, water, cinnamon, cloves, port, orange peel and lemon peel to simmer. Add pears and cook for about 20 to 25 minutes or until pears are tender. Remove pears from liquid and chill. Continue cooking liquid until it becomes a light syrupy consistency; chill. To serve, spoon syrup over pears.

Makes 4 servings.

Roast Goose

This makes an elegant and always-special meal.

1 goose (9 to 10 lb.)
1½ cups chicken broth
1½ tablespoons cornstarch

Prick skin of goose every few inches with tines of a sharp fork. Tie legs and tail together and place goose on a rack in an open roasting pan. Roast goose for 3 to 4 hours or until meat thermometer reaches 190° F. Remove goose to warm platter.

To make gravy, remove as much fat from roasting pan as possible. Stir chicken broth into pan drippings and juices. Pour this liquid into a saucepan and bring to a simmer. Gradually stir in cornstarch which has been mixed with ¼ cup cold water. Cook until mixture thickens. Serve with goose.

Makes 8 to 10 servings.

Red Cabbage with Apples

An ideal rich accompaniment to roast goose or roast pork.

3 tablespoons butter or margarine
3 medium apples, peeled and thinly sliced
1 small head red cabbage (1½ to 2 lbs.), thinly shredded
3 tablespoons sugar
¼ cup red wine vinegar
⅓ cup water
¼ teaspoon salt

In a large saucepan, melt butter. Add apples and sauté for 3 minutes. Add cabbage, sugar, vinegar, water and salt; stir. Cover and continue cooking over moderate heat for about 30 to 40 minutes, stirring occasionally.

Makes 4 servings.

Potato Pancakes

Once potatoes have been shredded, pancakes must be fried so that raw potatoes do not turn brown.

4 medium potatoes, peeled
1 tablespoon grated onion
2 eggs, slightly beaten
2 tablespoons flour
1 teaspoon salt
vegetable oil

Shred potatoes into a large bowl. Stir in onion, egg, flour and salt. Heat oil to a depth of about ⅛ inch in a heavy frying pan. Using about ⅓ cup batter for each pancake, drop potato mixture into hot oil. Brown pancakes on both sides; drain. Cooked pancakes may be kept in a warm oven while the remainder are fried.

Makes 4 to 6 servings.

Green and White Salad

The fixings are endless for a green and white salad. Simply select from ingredients already at home and improvise.

1 head romaine, washed and crisped
1 small head cauliflower, broken into flowerets
1 medium zucchini, thinly sliced
1 cup sliced fresh mushrooms

Tear romaine into bite-size pieces and place in a salad bowl. Add cauliflower, zucchini and mushrooms. Toss gently; chill. Top with a favorite dressing and serve.

Makes 4 to 6 servings.

MENU

Roast Goose

Red Cabbage with Apples

Potato Pancakes

Green and White Salad

Mocha Iced Layer Cake

Mocha Iced Layer Cake

For best results, the cake should be baked a day before slicing and icing.

1 package (18.5 oz.) butter recipe golden cake mix
1½ lb. butter, softened and divided
3 eggs
2 egg yolks
4 tablespoons cocoa
1 cup sugar, divided
2 tablespoons strong coffee
¼ cup dark rum, divided
1 tablespoon flour
¾ cup milk
1 teaspoon vanilla extract

Prepare cake mix according to package directions, using ¼ lb. butter and 3 eggs. Pour into a 9" x 13" baking pan and bake as directed.

In a small saucepan over moderate heat, bring ½ cup water, 2 tablespoons sugar and 3 tablespoons rum to boil. Stir until sugar is dissolved; remove from heat and cool.

In a bowl of the mixer, beat together 1 lb. butter with cocoa, 5 tablespoons sugar, coffee and remaining rum; refrigerate.

In a saucepan, stir together egg yolks and remaining sugar. Stir in flour; then beat in milk and vanilla. Place over low heat and cook, stirring continuously until mixture thickens. Cool thoroughly. Add this mixture to the butter mixture and mix well to make the frosting.

Carefully cut the cake into 5 layers. Place the bottom layer on a serving plate. Brush with some of the rum syrup; then spread with some of the frosting. Repeat until all layers are completed. With remaining frosting, ice sides and top of cake. Refrigerate cake if prepared long before serving. Bring to room temperature to serve.

Makes 1 (9" x 13") cake.

Smoked Pork Loin

Smoked pork has a rich flavor and should be served thinly sliced.

1 (2 lb.) smoked pork center-loin roast

Place pork loin on a rack in an open roasting pan. Roast at 325° F. for 1½ hours or until meat thermometer reaches 170° F. Let roast rest for 10 to 15 minutes before carving.

Makes 6 servings.

Potatoes and Parsnips Anna

An especially handsome company dish when unmolded or it may be served from the casserole.

¼ lb. butter or margarine, melted
3 to 4 large boiling potatoes (1½ lbs.)
¾ teaspoon salt
½ lb. parsnips, peeled and thinly sliced lengthwise
¼ teaspoon ground pepper

Preheat oven to 450° F.

Pour clear yellow butter liquid into a small saucepan and warm. Discard milky residue. Peel and cut potatoes into very thin slices; dry slices thoroughly. Peel parsnips and cut into very thin lengthwise slices.

Pour thin layer of butter into bottom of a 2-quart shallow, heavy casserole. Neatly arrange a layer of overlapping potato slices on bottom of dish. Pour a few tablespoons of butter over potatoes; sprinkle with some salt and pepper. Arrange a layer of parsnips over potatoes; top with butter and then salt and pepper. Repeat layers, ending with potatoes. Press potatoes and parsnips down into casserole. Cover with tight-fitting lid and bake for 20 minutes. Remove from oven, uncover and again press potatoes and parsnips down. Bake for an additional 20 minutes, uncovered.

To serve, invert casserole onto a hot serving platter. Or vegetables may be served in the casserole dish.

Makes 4 servings.

Pan Fried Spinach

Spinach should be cooked just before serving and only until it is barely wilted.

1½ tablespoons butter or margarine
2 lbs. spinach, washed and stems trimmed
¾ teaspoon Worcestershire sauce
2 teaspoons lemon juice
¼ teaspoon salt
dash ground pepper

Melt butter in a fry pan over moderate heat. Add spinach; stir, cooking, until spinach has barely wilted. Add Worcestershire, lemon juice, salt and pepper. Stir again and cook for an additional minute.

Makes 4 servings.

Sweet and Sour Cherry Tomatoes

This recipe has a mild sweet and sour flavor that is enhanced by the use of tarragon.

2 tablespoons sugar
2 tablespoons water
3 tablespoons wine vinegar
¼ cup vegetable oil
½ teaspoon dried leaf tarragon
¼ teaspoon salt
⅛ teaspoon ground pepper
1 lb. cherry tomatoes, washed and halved

In a small saucepan, heat sugar and water over moderately high heat until mixture comes to boil and sugar is dissolved. Remove from heat and pour into a bowl. Add vinegar, oil, tarragon, salt and pepper. Stir and allow mixture to cool to room temperature. Place cherry tomatoes in another bowl. Pour liquid over tomatoes and toss gently. Cover and refrigerate for at least 8 hours, stirring 2 or 3 times while tomatoes are marinating.

Makes 4 servings.

Apple Strudel

Be sure to keep prepared filo/strudel dough well covered so that it does not become brittle while making this dessert.

4 cups apple slices
⅓ cup sugar
½ teaspoon ground cinnamon
¼ teaspoon ground nutmeg
¼ cup seedless raisins or currants
3 pieces prepared filo/strudel dough
4 tablespoons butter or margarine, melted
2 tablespoons fine, dry bread crumbs

In a bowl, toss together apple slices, sugar, cinnamon, nutmeg and raisins; set aside.

Place 1 sheet of filo dough on piece of waxed paper which is a bit larger than dough. Brush sheet of dough with butter and sprinkle with a tablespoon of bread crumbs. Cover with another piece of dough; again brush with butter and sprinkle with crumbs. Top with remaining piece of dough. Place apple slice mixture in 3-inch wide strip at long edge of dough. Using waxed paper, roll up strudel, making sure filling stays inside of dough. Place rolled strudel on buttered baking sheet. Bake for 35 minutes at 350° F.

Makes 6 servings.

Double Decker Baked Fish

For this recipe, purchase fish in 1 piece rather than buying small fillets.

4 tablespoons butter or margarine
1½ cups fresh sliced mushrooms
¾ cup herb seasoned stuffing mix
1 tablespoon fresh lime juice
2 tablespoons water
1 lb. fish fillet (haddock, cod or similar fish)

In a fry pan, melt butter over moderate heat. Add mushrooms and sauté until mushrooms are tender; remove from heat. In a bowl, stir together mushrooms, stuffing mix, lime juice and water; set aside.

Cut piece of fish in half crosswise. Place stuffing on 1 piece of fish. Top with other piece of fish. Place on a buttered baking sheet. Bake at 375° F. for 20 to 25 minutes or until fish flakes easily with a fork. Cut into 4 pieces and serve.

Makes 4 servings.

Green Beans with Pecans

A delicious change from this vegetable frequently served with almonds.

1 lb. fresh green beans
3 tablespoons butter or margarine
⅓ cup coarsely chopped pecans

Rinse and cut green beans into 1-inch lengths. Cook beans in boiling salted water until tender.

Meanwhile, in a frying pan, melt butter. Sauté pecans in butter until lightly toasted.

To serve, toss green beans with sautéed pecans and butter.

Makes 4 servings.

Squash Soufflé

A light, elegant way to serve this everyday vegetable.

4 tablespoons butter or margarine
5 tablespoons flour
¾ cup milk
¼ teaspoon salt
¼ teaspoon ground nutmeg
2 cups cooked, mashed fresh winter squash
3 tablespoons brown sugar
4 eggs, separated

Preheat oven to 375° F. In a large saucepan, melt butter. Stir in flour and cook over moderate heat for about 5 minutes, without browning flour. Beat in milk, salt and nutmeg and allow to come to boil; remove from heat. Stir in squash and brown sugar. Then stir in egg yolks one at a time; set aside. In a bowl, beat egg whites until stiff, not dry. Fold egg whites quickly into squash mixture. Spoon into a buttered 1½-quart soufflé dish. Bake for 40 to 45 minutes.

Makes 6 servings.

Molded Cranberry Salad

Here is just the festive touch for a holiday dinner.

1 package (3 oz.) lemon-flavored gelatin
1 package (3 oz.) raspberry-flavored gelatin
2 cups boiling water
1 cup cold water
1 orange, halved and seeded
1 apple, peeled, halved and seeded
1 pound fresh cranberries
1 cup sugar

Pour gelatin into large bowl. Add boiling water and stir until gelatin is dissolved. Add cold water and stir; set aside. Grind orange, apple and cranberries into bowl. Stir in sugar. Add fruit mixture to gelatin mixture. Pour cranberry-gelatin mixture into 8-cup mold. Refrigerate until set. Unmold to serve.

Makes 10 servings.

Heavenly Hash Pudding

Now that same great candy flavor in pudding.

1 package (3⅝ oz.) chocolate pudding and pie filling
2 cups milk
1 cup miniature marshmallows or 12 marshmallows, quartered
⅓ cup coarsely chopped almonds

Prepare chocolate pudding according to package directions, using milk. Allow pudding to cool for 5 minutes. Stir in marshmallows and nuts. Pour into serving container. Chill.

Makes 4 servings.

Braised Brisket of Beef

This meat is delicious served with its natural cooking juices.

2 tablespoons vegetable oil
1 (3 lb.) beef brisket
2 medium onions, sliced
2 carrots, peeled and sliced
1 garlic clove, minced
1 cup sliced fresh mushrooms
⅔ cup beef consommé
½ teaspoon salt
⅛ teaspoon ground pepper

In a large saucepan, heat oil over moderately high heat. Add brisket and brown well on all sides; remove from pan. Add onions, carrots and garlic. Reduce heat to moderate and cook until onions are transparent. Return meat to pan. Add mushrooms, consommé, salt and pepper. Cover and simmer for 1½ to 2 hours or until meat is tender. Carve and serve meat with pan juices and vegetables.

Makes 4 to 6 servings.

Kasha with Egg Bow Noodles

An interesting and delicious break from potatoes or rice.

¼ cup small egg bow noodles
1 egg, slightly beaten
1 cup kasha (buckwheat groats)
2 cups beef consommé, hot
2 tablespoons butter or margarine

Cook egg bow noodles in a saucepan according to package directions; drain. Meanwhile, in a bowl, stir together egg and kasha; pour mixture into a fry pan and place over moderately high heat. Stir continuously for 2 to 3 minutes or until kasha grains are dry and separated. Add consommé and butter. Cover pan tightly and reduce heat to simmer. Cook for 15 to 20 minutes or until tender and all liquid is absorbed. Stir in hot egg bows.

Makes 6 servings.

Baked Tarragon Carrots

Select baked vegetables when you are planning an oven meal.

1 lb. carrots, peeled and cut into thick sticks
3 tablespoons butter or margarine, melted
½ teaspoon dried leaf tarragon
½ teaspoon salt

Place carrots in 1½-quart casserole. Add butter, tarragon and salt; mix well. Bake at 350° F. for 35 to 40 minutes, stirring once during baking.

Makes 4 servings.

Simple Sprouts

An easy way with a flavorful vegetable.

1 lb. Brussel sprouts
¼ cup grated Parmesan cheese
3 tablespoons butter or margarine, melted

In a saucepan, cook Brussel sprouts in rapidly boiling salted water until tender; drain. Toss quickly with cheese and butter.

Makes 4 servings.

Romaine and Orange Salad

The combination of citrus fruit and greens makes an extra-moist, interesting salad.

1 head romaine lettuce, washed and crisped
3 oranges, peeled and sectioned
2 tablespoons wine vinegar
6 tablespoons vegetable oil
1 teaspoon poppy seeds
½ teaspoon salt
⅛ teaspoon ground pepper

Tear lettuce into bite-size pieces; place in bowl. Gently toss orange sections with lettuce; chill. In a small bowl, beat together vinegar, oil, poppy seeds, salt and pepper. Pour over salad.

Makes 6 servings.

Honey Baked Apples

Serve baked apples still warm with light cream or ice cream.

4 medium cooking apples, cored
½ cup honey
½ teaspoon ground cinnamon
¼ cup seedless raisins
2 tablespoons butter or margarine

Place apples in a baking dish. Drizzle with honey and sprinkle with cinnamon. Fill cavity with raisins and a pat of butter. Bake at 350° F. for about 45 minutes or until apples are tender.

Makes 4 servings.

Veal Paprika

If boneless veal is not available at the market, buy a bone-in cut and make your own cubes of veal.

3 tablespoons vegetable oil
2 lbs. boneless veal, cut into 1-inch pieces
2 medium onions, thinly sliced
1 tablespoon paprika
1½ teaspoons salt
1 cup chicken broth
1 tablespoon flour
2 tablespoons dry white wine or dry vermouth
16 fresh mushroom buttons
2 tablespoons butter or margarine
½ cup sour cream

In a sauce pot, heat oil over moderate heat. Add veal and cook until meat is well browned on all sides. Remove meat from pot and add onion, paprika and salt, cooking until onion is tender. Return meat to pot and pour in chicken broth. Bring to simmer and cook, covered, for about 1½ to 2 hours or until meat is tender.

Meanwhile, in a small bowl, beat together flour and white wine; set aside. Sauté mushrooms in butter over moderate heat until tender. Add mushrooms to cooked veal. Stir flour-wine mixture into cooking liquid and simmer until liquid thickens. Stir in sour cream and serve immediately.

Makes 6 servings.

Poppy Seeded Noodles

If you don't want to cook the noodles at the last minute, spoon prepared noodles into a buttered, covered casserole and place in a 250° F. oven to hold for a short time.

1 package (8 oz.) wide egg noodles
3 tablespoons butter or margarine, melted
¼ cup chopped fresh chives
1 tablespoon poppy seeds

Prepare noodles according to package directions. Drain and place in serving bowl. Pour butter over noodles and sprinkle with chives and poppy seeds. Gently toss.

Makes 4 servings.

Broccoli Sesame

Try this easy and quick topping for fresh broccoli.

**1 bunch fresh broccoli (about 1½ lbs.), cleaned and
    trimmed into spears
1 tablespoon sesame seeds
¼ teaspoon salt**

Cook broccoli in rapidly boiling salted water until tender;
drain. Meanwhile, preheat broiler. Place sesame seeds on
baking sheet and place in oven. Toast sesame seeds under
broiler, watching continuously to be sure that sesames don't
burn. Sprinkle sesame seeds and salt over cooked broccoli.

Makes 4 servings.

Marinated Cucumbers

*Chopped dill weed makes a delicious garnish for this cucum-
ber salad.*

**2 large cucumbers, peeled and thinly sliced
2 teaspoons salt
⅓ cup vinegar
2 teaspoons sugar
1 tablespoon minced onion
¼ teaspoon ground pepper
lettuce leaves**

Place cucumbers and salt in a shallow bowl. Toss and allow
to sit for 1 to 2 hours. Rinse, wipe dry and place in a clean
bowl. In another bowl, stir together vinegar, sugar, onion
and pepper; pour over cucumbers. Stir and allow to sit,
refrigerated for 2 to 3 hours. To serve, drain off nearly all
liquid and place cucumbers on lettuce leaves.

Makes 4 servings.

MENU

Veal Paprika
Poppy Seeded Noodles
Broccoli Sesame
Marinated Cucumbers
Cream Puff Ring

Cream Puff Ring

To be sure that the cream puff ring is a perfect circle, mark baking sheet with an 8-inch round cake pan as a guide.

Puff Ring:

1 cup water
½ cup butter or margarine
¼ teaspoon salt
2 teaspoons sugar
1 cup flour
4 eggs

In a saucepan over high heat, bring water, butter, salt and sugar to a boil. Reduce heat to low and beat in flour vigorously with a spoon until mixture forms a ball and leaves sides of pan. Remove from heat. Beat eggs into flour mixture, one at a time. Spoon mixture into a pastry bag fitted with a tube having ½-inch opening. Butter and flour a baking sheet. Squeeze dough onto sheet in an 8-inch circle to make one ring. Then squeeze another ring on top of the first ring, so that the dough is 2 layers high. Bake in a preheated 400° F. oven for about 25 minutes. Cool.

Filling and Topping:

½ cup sugar
¼ cup cornstarch
¼ teaspoon salt
2 cups milk
2 eggs, slightly beaten
1 tablespoon vanilla extract
¾ cup chocolate sauce

In a saucepan, stir together sugar, cornstarch and salt. Stir in milk and cook, stirring continuously, over moderate heat. Cook for about 10 minutes or until mixture thickens. In a bowl, stir ¼ of the hot milk mixture into eggs, then pour egg mixture slowly back into the milk mixture, stirring continuously. Stir in vanilla and cool. Refrigerate until mixture is cold.

To assemble: Slice cream puff ring in half horizontally, lifting off top ring. Remove any soft dough inside of rings. Fill with filling mixture. Replace top of ring. Spoon chocolate sauce over ring and serve.

Makes 8 servings.

Note: When not using a pastry bag, simply spoon ring mixture into 8-inch circle.

Escarole Soup with Meatballs

Serve soup with grated Parmesan cheese and chopped tomatoes.

½ lb. ground beef
½ cup fine, dry bread crumbs
¼ cup grated Parmesan cheese
¼ cup minced onion
2 eggs, slightly beaten
2 garlic cloves, minced
½ teaspoon dried leaf oregano
½ teaspoon salt
⅛ teaspoon crushed hot red pepper
3½ cups chicken broth
2 carrots, peeled and chopped
4 cups escarole, washed and torn into small pieces

In a bowl, stir together ground beef, crumbs, cheese, onion, eggs, garlic, oregano, salt and pepper. Shape into 16 small meatballs. Brown meatballs in a fry pan or bake in oven until done.

Meanwhile, heat chicken broth to simmer. Add carrots and cook until tender. Stir in cooked meatballs and escarole. Cover and simmer until escarole is wilted and just tender.

Makes 4 servings.

MENU

Escarole Soup with Meatballs

Eggplant Parmigiana

Linguini with Garlic Butter

Ricotta Rum Cake

Eggplant Parmigiana

Try doubling this recipe and then freezing half (before baking) for another meal.

1 medium eggplant (about 1¼ lbs.)
2½ teaspoons salt, divided
2 tablespoons vegetable oil
1 large onion, peeled and chopped
2 garlic cloves, peeled and minced
2 cups fresh mushroom slices
1 can (28 oz.) peeled Italian-style tomatoes, crushed
1 teaspoon dried leaf oregano
1 teaspoon dried leaf basil
3 bay leaves
⅛ teaspoon crushed red pepper
2 eggs, slightly beaten
2 tablespoons water
¼ cup flour
½ cup fine, dry bread crumbs
6 tablespoons grated Parmesan cheese
oil for frying
1½ cups shredded mozzarella cheese

Peel and slice eggplant horizontally about ½-inch thick. Sprinkle on both sides with 2 teaspoons salt and place on a baking sheet.

Heat oil in a large saucepan over moderate heat. Add onion, garlic and mushrooms; cook until onion is tender. Add tomatoes, oregano, basil, salt, bay leaves and red pepper. Stir well; cover pan and simmer tomato sauce for about 1 hour. Remove cover and continue cooking until sauce thickens; remove from heat.

Pat eggplant dry. In a shallow bowl, beat together eggs and water. Place flour in another shallow bowl. In a third shallow bowl, stir together crumbs and 4 tablespoons Parmesan cheese. Dip eggplant slices first in flour, then in egg mixture and finally in crumbs to bread. Fry in hot oil until golden brown; drain.

Spoon a thin layer of tomato sauce into a 1½ quart casserole. Top with a layer of eggplant slices and sprinkle with ⅓ cup mozzarella cheese. Repeat layers twice, ending with remaining tomato sauce. Then sprinkle with remaining mozzarella cheese. Top with 2 tablespoons Parmesan cheese. Bake at 350° F. for 35 to 40 minutes or until cheese is browned and tomato sauce is bubbly.

Makes 4 servings.

Linguini with Garlic Butter

Cook linguini until it is "al dente" — still a little firm in texture.

12 oz. linguini or spaghetti
¼ cup butter
2 garlic cloves, minced
1 tablespoon minced parsley

Cook linguini according to package directions; drain. Meanwhile, melt butter in a saucepan over moderate heat. Add garlic and stir until garlic just begins to brown. Remove pan from heat and stir in parsley. Pour garlic butter over drained linguini and toss gently.

Makes 6 servings.

Ricotta Rum Cake

Here's the kind of dessert that can be prepared in just 10 minutes and it will keep refrigerated for several hours before serving.

1 (10¾ oz.) frozen pound cake, thawed
⅔ cup heavy cream
¼ cup powdered sugar
⅓ cup ricotta cheese
⅓ cup semi-sweet chocolate bits, finely chopped
3 tablespoons dark rum

Slice pound cake horizontally into 3 layers. In a mixer bowl, whip cream with powdered sugar. Spoon half of the whipped cream into another bowl and stir in ricotta cheese, ¼ cup chopped chocolate and 1 tablespoon rum.

Place bottom layer of cake on serving plate. Brush cake with 1 tablespoon rum. Spoon half of ricotta mixture on top of cake. Repeat with next layer of cake. Cover with top of cake. Spoon remaining whipped cream over top of cake. Spread with knife to smooth. Sprinkle with remaining chopped chocolate. Refrigerate, covered, until time of serving.

Makes 6 to 8 servings.

MENU

Escarole Soup with Meatballs

Eggplant Parmigiana

Linguini with Garlic Butter

Ricotta Rum Cake

Sauerbraten with Gingersnap Gravy

When planning to serve sauerbraten, remember that the meat needs to marinate for 2 to 3 days before cooking.

⅔ cup dry red wine
⅔ cup red wine vinegar
⅔ cup water
3 bay leaves
10 peppercorns
2 medium onions, peeled and thinly sliced
1 tablespoon sugar
1 (4 lb.) eye of the round roast
3 tablespoons vegetable oil
¼ cup chopped celery
⅔ cup fine gingersnap crumbs

In a large bowl, stir together wine, vinegar, water, bay leaves, peppercorns, 1 sliced onion, and sugar. Add roast to marinade, cover and refrigerate for 2 to 3 days, turning meat at least twice a day.

Remove meat from marinade and pat dry with toweling. Strain and reserve marinade. Heat oil in a large sauce pot over moderate heat. Add meat and brown well on all sides; remove from pot. Pour off all but 1 tablespoon drippings. Add remaining onion and celery; cook over moderate heat until onions are tender. Sprinkle flour over vegetables and cook, stirring frequently for 5 minutes. Pour in reserved marinade and heat to boiling. Return meat to pot, reduce heat to simmer. Cook, covered, for about 2 hours or until meat is tender. Remove meat and place on a warm platter.

To make gravy, strain cooking liquid into a large measuring cup; skim off fat. There should be about 2 cups of liquid. If necessary add beef broth to make up the 2 cups. In a small saucepan, stir together liquid and gingersnap crumbs; bring to simmer and cook until sauce thickens. Spoon gingersnap gravy over carved meat.

Makes 6 to 8 servings.

Hungarian Cabbage and Noodles

Here's a delicious taste and texture combination of noodles and vegetable.

1 small green cabbage (1½ lbs.)
4 tablespoons butter or margarine
1 teaspoon salt
¼ teaspoon ground pepper
¼ lb. egg noodles

Melt butter in a large fry pan.

Remove and discard outer wilted cabbage leaves. Shred cabbage and place in a fry pan over moderate heat. Cook cabbage with salt and pepper, stirring periodically. Meanwhile, cook noodles in rapidly boiling salted water; drain. Add noodles to cabbage and stir together well. Continue to cook for an additional 5 minutes.

Makes 4 to 6 servings.

Green Peas with Bacon

For convenience, you may want to buy real bacon bits — ready to use.

3 lbs. fresh peas in the shell
6 strips bacon

Shell peas and cook in a saucepan in rapidly boiling salted water; drain. Meanwhile, in a fry pan over moderate heat, cook bacon. Remove bacon from the pan and drain off all but 2 tablespoons bacon drippings; set the pan aside. Finely chop bacon.

When peas are cooked, place them in the fry pan with bacon drippings and sauté briefly over moderate heat. Sprinkle with bacon crumbles.

Makes 4 servings.

MENU

Sauerbraten with Gingersnap gravy

Hungarian Cabbage and Noodles

Green Peas with Bacon

Pickled Beets and Onions

Blueberry Turnovers

Pickled Beets and Onions

An all-time favorite.

2 bunches fresh beets
1 small onion, thinly sliced
½ cup cider vinegar
5 tablespoons sugar
½ teaspoon dry mustard
½ teaspoon ground clove
½ teaspoon salt

Cook beets in rapidly boiling lightly salted water. Drain beets reserving 1 cup cooking liquid. Peel and slice. Place beets in a bowl with onion slices; set aside. In another bowl, stir together beets and onions. Mix thoroughly. Refrigerate for 1 to 2 days before serving, stirring once or twice.

Makes 6 servings.

Blueberry Turnovers

Be sure to seal edges of dough together well to hold in turnover filling.

1 can (15 oz.) blueberries, drained
3 tablespoons sugar
2 tablespoons flour
1 teaspoon lemon juice
⅛ teaspoon ground cinnamon
⅛ teaspoon ground nutmeg
1 package (17¼ oz.) frozen puff pastry sheets, thawed

In a bowl, stir together blueberries, sugar, flour, lemon juice, cinnamon and nutmeg; set aside.

Unwrap pastry sheets and cut each sheet in quarters by making diagonal cuts. Place a spoonful of blueberry mixture in centers of 4 pieces of pastry. Cover each with remaining 4 pieces of pastry. Pinch edges well to seal in filling. Place on baking sheet. Bake at 400° F. for 20 minutes.

Makes 4 large turnovers.

Mexican Chicken

Green chilies and coriander flavor this distinctive — though not hot — chicken dish.

4 tablespoons vegetable oil
1 (2 to 3 lb.) broiler-fryer chicken, cut in parts
1 medium onion, thinly sliced
1 can (16 oz.) peeled tomatoes, crushed
1 can (3 oz.) whole green chilies, drained, seeded and
    chopped
1 tablespoon lime juice
1 teaspoon dried coriander leaves
½ teaspoon salt

In a large fry pan, heat oil over moderately high heat. Brown chicken well in 2 tablespoons oil. Drain off pan drippings.

Meanwhile, in a saucepan, heat remaining oil over moderate heat. Add onion and cook until tender. Add tomatoes, chilies, lime juice, coriander and salt. Simmer for 10 minutes. Spoon tomato mixture over browned chicken and cover. Cook over low heat for about 45 minutes. Remove chicken from pan and keep warm. Bring cooking liquid to a boil over high heat and reduce the amount of liquid to about ⅔ cup. Return chicken to the fry pan, reduce heat to simmer and cook for another 5 minutes.

Makes 4 servings.

MENU

Mexican Chicken
Refried Beans
Avocado and Citrus Salad
Flan

Refried Beans

Simplify the recipe, if you wish, by using 2 (15 ounce) cans of pinto beans in place of dried beans.

1 lb. dried pinto beans
5 cups water
½ cup bacon drippings, butter or lard
¾ cup chopped onion
1 can (3 oz.) green chilies, chopped
2 medium tomatoes, peeled, seeded and coarsely chopped
1 teaspoon salt

In a large pot, stir together beans and water. Bring to a boil, cover and remove from heat for 2 hours or overnight. Return to heat, bringing to a boil and simmer slowly until beans are very tender or about 3 hours. Mash beans with a potato masher.

In a large heavy fry pan, melt bacon drippings. Add onion, chilies and tomatoes, cooking until onion is transparent. Add mashed beans and salt. Cook over low heat, stirring frequently for about 5 to 10 minutes.

Makes 6 servings.

Avocado and Citrus Salad

If you're preparing the salad long before serving time, dip avocado slices in citrus juice.

1 head Boston lettuce, washed and crisped
1 ripe avocado, peeled
1 orange, peeled and sectioned
1 grapefruit, peeled and sectioned

Line serving plates with lettuce leaves. Cut avocado into thin slices. Arrange avocado slices alternately with citrus slices on top of lettuce. Chill.

Makes 4 servings.

Flan

A smooth, cool Mexican baked custard.

¾ **cup suger, divided**
3 eggs
¼ **teaspoon salt**
1 cup milk
1 cup light cream
1 teaspoon vanilla extract

In a small, heavy saucepan, over moderate heat, melt ½ cup sugar, stirring constantly until it is light brown in color. Pour immediately into buttered custard cups or a baking dish; set aside.

In a large bowl, beat together eggs and remaining sugar until mixture is lemon-colored. Gradually beat in milk, cream and vanilla. Pour into caramel-lined baking dish(es). Place dish(es) in a pan of boiling water and bake at 350° F. for about 40 minutes or until knife inserted off-center comes out clean. Allow custard to cool and then refrigerate until well chilled. To unmold, loosen edge of custard and invert onto a serving dish.

Makes 4 servings.

MENU

Mexican Chicken
Refried Beans
Avocado and Citrus Salad
Flan

Corn Chowder

Here's a hearty soup that can be made in just fifteen minutes.

2 tablespoons butter or margarine
½ cup chopped onion
2 medium potatoes, peeled, diced and cooked
2 cups milk
1 can (17 oz.) cream style corn
½ teaspoon salt
⅛ teaspoon ground pepper

In a saucepan over moderate heat, melt butter. Stir in onion and sauté until onion is transparent. Add potatoes. Stir in milk, corn, salt and pepper. Bring to simmer and cook, stirring continuously for 5 minutes.

Makes 4 servings.

Build a Burger

Here's a way that diners have fun with a do-it-yourself meal.

1½ lbs. ground beef
2 tablespoons vegetable oil
1 medium onion, peeled and sliced
1 medium green pepper, seeded and sliced
2 tablespoons butter or margarine
6 fresh mushrooms, sliced
¼ lb. grated Cheddar cheese
2 medium tomatoes, sliced
6 hamburger rolls

Shape ground beef into 6 patties and broil to desired degree of doneness. Meanwhile, in a fry pan, heat oil. Add onions and peppers, cooking until onions are tender. In another fry pan, melt butter over moderate heat. Add mushrooms and cook until tender.

Place cooked onion-pepper mixture in one bowl; place mushrooms in another bowl. Place cheese and tomatoes in separate bowls. Serve cooked burgers and allow guests to build their own burgers from the selection of toppings.

Makes 6 servings.

Homemade French Fries

For potato chips, simply cut potatoes into thin slices and cook just like French fries.

4 medium potatoes
vegetable oil
salt

Peel potatoes and cut into sticks. Dry potatoes thoroughly. Heat oil in deep saucepan to 390° F. to 400° F. Gently lower a few potatoes at a time into hot oil. Fry for 5 minutes or until golden brown; drain. Repeat with remaining potatoes. Sprinkle with salt to taste and serve immediately.

Makes 4 servings.

Artichokes and Mushrooms à la Grecque

This recipe makes a perfect first course, may be mixed with salad greens for a tossed salad, or may be served alone as a salad.

¼ cup olive oil
1 medium onion, chopped
1 carrot, peeled and finely chopped
⅓ cup dry white wine or dry vermouth
½ lb. fresh mushroom buttons
2 bay leaves
1 garlic clove, minced
½ teaspoon salt
⅛ teaspoon ground pepper
1 can (14 oz.) artichoke hearts, drained and halved
2 tablespoons chopped parsley

In a saucepan, heat oil over moderate heat. Add onion and carrot, cooking until onion is soft. Add wine and simmer for 2 minutes. Add mushrooms, bay leaves, garlic, salt and pepper. Simmer uncovered for 7 to 10 minutes, stirring occasionally. Remove from heat; add artichokes. Place mixture in bowl and cool. Refrigerate for at least 3 hours before serving. Sprinkle with parsley.

Makes 4 to 6 servings.

Cherry Crisp

Try serving cherry crisp a la mode with your choice of ice cream flavors.

¼ cup butter or margarine
½ cup brown sugar
½ cup flour
1 can (21 oz.) cherry pie filling
⅛ teaspoon almond extract
½ cup heavy cream, whipped

In a bowl, blend together butter, brown sugar and flour; set aside. In another bowl, stir together pie filling and almond extract. Spoon into an 8-inch square baking dish. Sprinkle top with flour mixture. Bake at 350° F. for 20 to 25 minutes. Cool. Top with whipped cream or ice cream.

Makes 4 servings.

Index